The Illustrated
RULES
of
GOLF

The Illustrated
RULES
of
GOLF

Martin Vousden

WARD LOCK

Acknowledgements

We would like to thank the following for their help in creating this book: Mark Shearman who took all the photographs in the book. Robin Mann from Finn Valley Golf Centre in Suffolk who appeared with Martin Vousden in the photographs. Stoke by Nayland Golf Club in Suffolk for kindly allowing us to photograph on their beautiful and challenging course.

Text © Martin Vousden
© Ward Lock Limited 1991

Editor: Heather Thomas
Art director: Al Rockall
Designer: Rolando Ugolini
Illustrations: Rolando Ugolini
Photographs: Mark Shearman

Text set by Ipswich Typographics Ltd
Printed and bound in Great Britain by the Bath Press.

British Library Cataloguing in Publication Data

Vousden, Martin
   The illustrated rules of golf.
   1. Golf
   I. Title
   796.35202022

ISBN 0-7063-6996-3

Contents

The first hole 8
Drawing lots and teeing off
Provisional ball
Stroke and distance

The second hole 13
Lost ball and unplayable ball

The third hole 18
Pitch marks and spike marks
Cleaning and replacing balls
The flagstick

The fourth hole 24
Water hazards

The fifth hole 30
Lateral water hazards

The sixth hole 36
Obstructions
Loose impediments

The seventh hole 41
Casual water
Relief without penalty

The eighth hole 46
Golf ettiquette

The ninth hole 50
Hazards

The tenth hole 50
Bunkers
Touching the ground in a hazard
Casual water in a bunker

The eleventh hole 60
Lost balls and identification
Taking up a stance
Moving a ball in play

The twelfth hole 65
Ball not in play on teeing ground
Ball moving at address

The thirteenth hole 69
Outside agency
Striking another ball on the green

The fourteenth hole 74
Accidentally breaking a rule
Deliberately breaking a rule
Dropping and placing
Cleaning the ball
Dropping the ball

The fifteenth hole 79
Ball in its own pitch mark
Ball on the wrong putting green

The sixteenth hole 82
Winter rules
Fixed sprinkler heads

The seventeenth hole 86
Seeking and giving advice
Practice on the course

The eighteenth hole 91
Maximum clubs in a bag

Index 93

Martin Vousden

Martin Vousden is a reporter on the staff of *Today's Golfer* Magazine in the UK. He writes regular features on the Rules of golf for the magazine. His great regret is that he did not take up golf until his late twenties, and he lives for the two days a year when he plays below his handicap of 18. He is married and lives in Peterborough, England.

Robin Mann

Robin Mann modelled in some of the photographs and helped advise on the Rules and their application. He is Director of Golf at Finn Valley Golf Centre near Ipswich in Suffolk. He has competed on the European Tour between 1975 and 1990 and was UK Club Professional Champion in 1985. He has been Suffolk Professional Champion seven times and has won the East Anglian Championship twice.

The first hole

Meet George. He is a keen golfer but struggling to get his handicap down below the twenties. Having only played for a couple of years he has concentrated all his efforts on improving his swing, with the result that he has learnt little or nothing about the Rules of golf.

However, at least he is lucky enough to have joined a golf club, and today he is about to play his first medal round at his new club. As luck would have it, he is paired with the club captain — a stickler for, and authority on, the Rules.

Drawing lots and teeing off

The two players tossed a coin to see who tees off first — as this is a medal competition, played under the full Rules of Golf, they must 'draw lots' **(Rule 10-2)**. The rules do not acknowledge the tradition of allowing the lower handicapper to go first, which is the way George usually plays.

The first tee was immediately outside the clubhouse and, having won the toss, George bent down to place his ball between the yellow tee markers. The captain pointed out that as they were playing in the medal, the white (or furthest back) tees were in use. The two players were among the last to tee off in the competition and because of heavy overnight rain the tee was muddy and bare in places, causing George some difficulty in finding a suitable spot to place his ball.

Once again the captain came to his aid, telling George that he could place his ball anywhere within a rectangle two club lengths back from the tee markers **(Section II: Definitions)**.

He could, if he chose, stand outside the markers, as long as his ball was teed up within their boundaries.

Opposite above: The teeing ground is a rectangle of two club lengths from the front and outside of the tee markers (Rule 11). If part of the ball is within these margins, it can be legally played.
Opposite below: A player may stand outside the teeing ground in order to play a ball that is within it.
Below: All four balls are legally teed up because all or part of them are within the rectangle of tee markers and two club lengths.

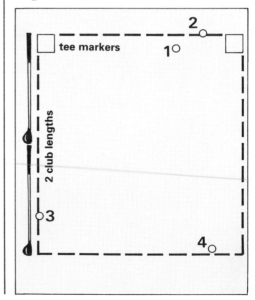

George teed his ball up, took a deep breath — and sliced straight into the trees on the right that also contained an out-of-bounds (OB) fence. He cursed his bad luck and stepped aside to let the captain play. Almost inevitably under the circumstances, he drove into the middle of the fairway.

Provisional ball

George grabbed his trolley handle and having said: "Good shot" was about to head in the direction of his ball when the captain asked: "Aren't you going to play a provisional?" **(Rule 27-2)**.

George was embarrassed to admit that he did not know what this was, so the captain explained: "If you play another, provisional, ball from here, and we cannot find your original, the provisional

Below: Ball 1 is legal because only part of it is out-of-bounds. However, ball 2 cannot be played as it lies.

becomes the ball in play. That way, you don't have to walk all the way back to the tee to play another shot. The provisional is, in effect, a safety net. If you find your first ball, fine; if you do not, you have already taken your next stroke without having to walk all the way back here."

If George had seen his first shot clearly travel out-of-bounds, he would have had no option but to play another ball because his first was irretrievable. Hitting the first ball would have counted as one stroke, he would receive a penalty stroke for going out-of-bounds and he would then hit the second ball. He would now be, in common golfing language, 'three off the tee'. Unfortunately, because he was still nervous, he topped the provisional shot, which only travelled 40 yards.

He was entitled to continue playing this

Below: The inside of the posts (golf-course side) is used to determine out-of-bounds. Ball 1 is legal but ball 2 cannot be played as it lies.

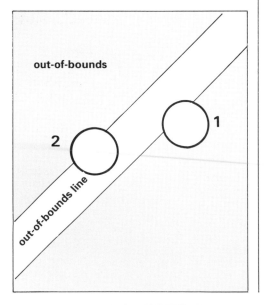

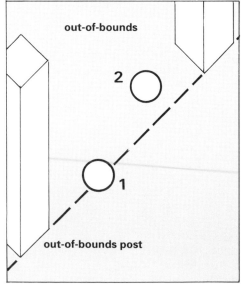

Above left: Having marked the limit of the two club lengths, the correct procedure for dropping is to stand erect with arm outstretched at shoulder height (Rule 20). If the ball touches the player, his partner, either of their caddies or equipment, it should be re-dropped without penalty, as many times as necessary.

Above right: If the ball strikes the ground within the permitted area, it may roll up to a further two club lengths away.

provisional ball until it reached, or passed, the point where his first disappeared **(Rule 27-2b)**. This it did on the next stroke (George's fourth), which he hit solidly with an iron club.

But before George went looking for his errant shot, one final word about putting a provisional ball in play. George had to say: "I am going to play a provisional ball", or very similar words **(Rule 27-2a)**. It is not enough to say: "I'd better hit another one", or: "Hang on, I'll just knock this one up the middle".

George eventually arrived at the spot where his ball disappeared and, to his delight, immediately found it. Therefore, he had to play it. He did not have the option of putting it in his pocket and continuing with the provisional ball. He could not, much as he might have liked to do so, declare the original ball lost once he had found it. What he could do, if he hit a good provisional ball and suspected that the original ball was in an unwelcome and difficult spot, was to continue playing the provisional without looking for the original. Of course, the quality of the shot he made with the provisional ball might affect the way he looked for the original, although this would be better illustrated perhaps with an example from a par 3 hole.

Imagine if George hit his first shot into an awful place, played a provisional ball and then hit that straight into the hole for a par three. He might well decide that even if he finds the original he is unlikely to get it into the hole in another two strokes. Therefore he makes only a cursory search of the bushes, or none at all. He has, in effect, paid the price of his misdemeanour by adding a penalty stroke to his score and if he should then happen to play a brilliant (or lucky) shot, so be it.

Stroke and distance

So on his opening hole in the medal competition, George had found his first tee shot in the trees. Without really weighing up the options he took a quick swipe and his elation of a minute before soon dissipated when he saw his ball heading straight for a tree trunk and then out-of-bounds. This time it was gone — he had no doubt because he saw it. The out-of-bounds line was clearly marked by white stakes.

He sheepishly asked the captain what he should do now. "You have only one course of action," he said. "You must play stroke and distance." Seeing George's puzzled look, he explained: "Stroke and distance means you take a one stroke penalty for losing the ball (stroke), and have to play your next shot from as near as possible to where you played the original one (distance). In this instance, right where you are standing **(Rule 27-1)**.

George therefore hit his tee shot into the woods, his second out-of-bounds, took a penalty shot for that offence and dropped another ball. The procedure is to stand with arm straight out, hand at shoulder height, and drop, as near as possible to the original spot but not nearer the hole **(Rule 20-2a)**. If it stays within two club lengths of that spot, no nearer the hole, it can be played *(see Chapter 2)*. He had now taken three strokes and played the remainder of the hole in four more. The captain made a par four.

Two further notes about out-of-bounds: if it is marked by stakes, the line of out-of-bounds is defined by the nearest inside points of the stakes or posts. If it is defined by a line on the ground, the line itself is OB and a ball is OB when all of it is OB.

■■■ Key points ■■■

1 If a ball is lost, the only option is stroke and distance.
2 If a ball goes out-of-bounds it is lost so the penalty is stroke and distance.
3 A provisional ball is a way of taking a stroke and distance penalty — if it should be needed — without having to walk back to the spot from which the original ball was played.
4 A ball once found must be played.
5 Out-of-bounds is marked by white stakes or lines.

The second hole

Having got the traumas of the first hole behind him, George was eager to get on with his round and proceeded enthusiastically to the second tee. This was the starting point of a 175 yard par 3 hole. Having scored better than George on the first hole, the captain now had 'the honour': that is, he plays first from the tee and will continue to do so until and unless George can better the captain's score on any hole.

The captain, in that sickeningly controlled way that George was already beginning to detest, hit a crisp iron to the heart of the green. George did not. Once again he sliced terribly, this time into deep rough. Before the captain could say a word, George declared: "I will play a provisional ball", and this time also found the green, albeit not as close as his playing partner.

Lost ball and unplayable ball

When both men reached the spot where they thought George's first ball went they put down their bags and proceeded to search. The captain asked: "What were you playing?" and George blushed scarlet and was forced to confess that he did not know. "I know I had a new Titleist on the first tee but when I lost it I grabbed the first ball I could from my bag and didn't check it. Oh, hang on, though, it's a Top Flite 3; I remember now because it was given to me by a friend who works in a bank and it has the bank's logo stamped on it."

Above: It is always advisable on the tee of any hole to make a mental note of the ball's make and number so that you can identify it later if necessary.

George was lucky. Had he not known which ball he was playing it would have been impossible to identify correctly any they found and his first ball would be lost **(Rule 27 Definition a)**. After two minutes' searching, another pair of golfers appeared on the tee behind them and the captain asked: "Shall we call them through?" George nodded and the captain waved to the other players to play the hole.

George knew that he was entitled to a five-minute search for his lost ball **(Rule 27a)** and thought the captain was being over-generous in waving through following players after only two minutes had elapsed. Sadly, this was a misconception he shared with many golfers. All of us have a responsibility to wave another match through immediately it is clear that we have to search, or that we are, for whatever reason, holding them up.

While the following golfers were playing through, George and the captain

found the ball but it was in a deep tangle of rough from which George knew he could never play it, so he asked the captain for advice and his answer was: "You have three choices if you decide that your ball is unplayable **(Rule 28)**. First, you can replay the shot from where

Below and opposite below: A player can declare his ball unplayable at any time unless it lies in or touches a water hazard (Rule 28). One of the options from an unplayable lie, under a one-stroke penalty, is to drop a ball within two club lengths of where it lay, but not nearer the hole. Here the player is measuring two club lengths using the longest club in his bag to gain the maximum distance.

you last hit it, taking a penalty stroke, which you now know is stroke and distance **(Rule 20-5)''**.

At this point George interrupted and said: "But haven't I already taken care of that by playing a provisional ball? You said that it is an insurance policy so can't I now elect the stroke and distance option and continue with my provisional ball, to save me all the bother of going back to the tee?''

"I'm afraid you can't," the captain replied. "You can only continue to play a provisional ball if your original is lost."

"OK," said George. "So what other choices do I have?''

"The second option is to drop your ball within two club lengths of where it came to rest, no nearer the hole. The third is to go back as far as you like in order to drop the ball, but you must keep the spot where it rests now between you and the hole."

Let us examine this more closely because it is probably one of the most abused rules in golf. Many players think that they should re-trace the flight of the ball into the spot where it becomes unplayable but this is not so. They should stand behind the ball, facing the flag, and go directly backwards until they find a spot where they want to drop.

It is up to the individual player to declare a ball unplayable, and he can do

this anywhere on the course, except if the ball is in or touches a water hazard *(see Chapters 4 and 5)*. It is also up to him and him alone to decide how far back to go before dropping his ball — if he selects this one of his three options. And if his ball is in a bunker, it must be dropped within the bunker.

In this instance George spotted an area of fairly smooth grass within two club lengths of his ball and so dropped within that area. His ball did not roll more than two club lengths, nor did it roll nearer the hole so it was an acceptable drop. Sadly, he played a poor shot that travelled about 80 yards before disappearing into a thicket of trees and bushes.

According to the Rules of Golf, there are three ways in which a ball may become lost outside a water hazard (for water hazards *see Chapters 4 and 5)*. They are:

● If another ball is put into play under the Rules.
● If the five-minute search time has elapsed.
● If the player continues play with a provisional ball from a spot where the original ball is likely to be or nearer the hole than that spot **(Rule 27)**.

The third solution sounds more complicated that it really is. When playing a provisional ball you are allowed to hit it as many times as necessary to get it to, or past, the point where your original ball is likely to be. But if it reaches that spot and you then play another stroke with the provisional ball you are, by your actions, declaring the original ball lost. To make a clear verbal declaration along the lines of: "I declare that ball lost (and good riddance!)" is actually meaningless in the Rules of Golf, which acknowledge only the above three ways of losing a ball.

For example, if a player hits his tee shot

into thick rough and simply tees up another, without saying: "I am going to play a provisional ball", he would, by his actions, be abandoning the original ball.

Opposite: This illustrates dropping from an unplayable lie. A player decides that his shot played here from the tee (1) is unplayable so he has three options, all under one-stroke penalty. He can go back to the tee and replay the stroke (stroke and distance), or he can drop within two club lengths of where the ball lay, not nearer the hole (2). Finally he can go back as far as he wants on a line that keeps the point where the ball lay between him and the hole (3) (Rule 28). If he selects the third, he must drop on the line, not to the side.

■■■■■■**Key points**■■■■■■

1 If you cannot identify your ball you have no option but to consider it lost.
2 A golfer may declare his ball unplayable at any time except if it is in a water hazard.
3 There are three options once a ball is declared unplayable:
● Stroke and distance.
● A drop within two club lengths (adding a penalty stroke to the score).
● A drop anywhere back on a line that keeps the spot where the ball came to rest between you and the hole (also for the addition of a penalty stroke).
4 If you declare a ball unplayable in a bunker, it must be dropped in the bunker.

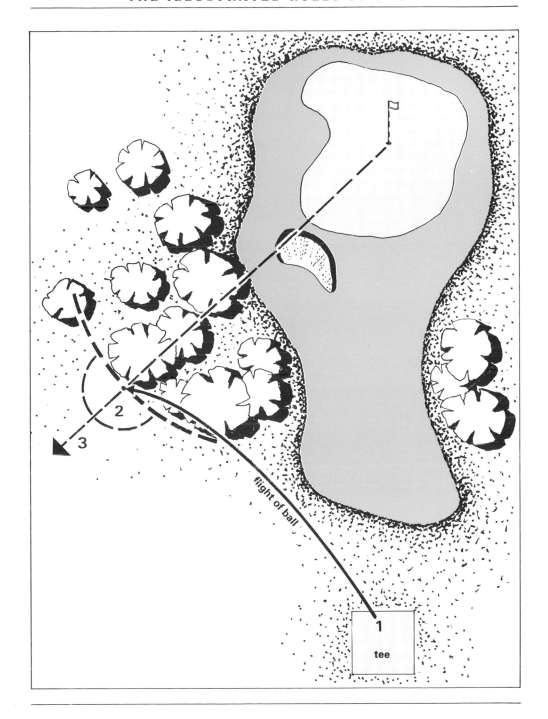

flight of ball

1
tee

2

3

The third hole

At the third hole, a 380 yard par 4, the captain again had the honour and pulled his shot just off the fairway left. George, who was beginning to wish he had taken up another sport instead of golf, lunged mightily and hit the ground behind the ball, taking a huge divot and propelling his ball about 60 yards. One of the things he had learned was always to replace divots but, as he bent down to do this, the captain quietly informed him that he should not do this on the tee.

George was uncertain until the captain explained: "It is not written in the Rules but it is generally accepted that it is potentially dangerous to replace divots here because someone else could stand on it and lose his footing if it should slip from under him as he plays his shot."

Pitch marks and spike marks

Both players proceeded to the green without incident, the captain taking a further two strokes and George taking four. His final approach was a bump-and-run shot from just off the green, whereas his partner (or 'fellow competitor' as the Rules would say in stroke play, and 'opponent' in match play), hit a 50 yard pitch that carried high and stopped almost dead on landing. When he first started playing, George could never remember the difference between a pitch and a chip; only knowing that one was floated high and the other struck on a much lower trajectory — in consequence, many instruction books and articles left him thoroughly bemused. Until, that is, another golfer told him to remember that: "We pitch up to the golf course and the chips go down".

Because the captain's ball dropped from a high approach, it left a pitch mark on the green which he proceeded to repair **(Rule 16-1c)**. George enquired about this, admitting that he was never quite sure what to do on the rare occasions when a full shot of his found the putting surface. The captain explained that the impact of the ball made a slight dent in the grass by pushing a small portion of it forward. The pitch mark repairer which he carries in his pocket is then used to lever that piece of grass back into position before he gently tamps it down with the sole of his putter.

Some golfers use the sole of their shoe to tamp the grass down but this is unhelpful because studded golf shoes can leave spike marks, which cannot be repaired before all the players have putted. This point caused some animosity between the Australian Brett Ogle and the Englishman Roger Chapman in the last European Tour event of the 1990 season, the Volvo Masters. Chapman holed out quickly and spun round before starting to walk away from the hole. Brett Ogle was irritated at the spike marks this caused and, as they were on the far side of the hole from where he was putting, he asked Chapman to tamp them down, which he did. However, as far as the R&A is concerned, the line of a putt extends through the hole and continues on the

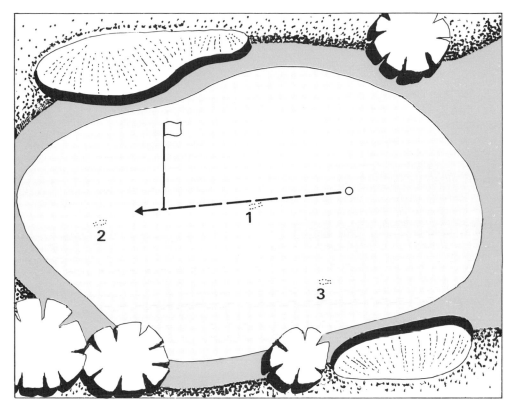

*Above: Spike mark **1** cannot be repaired as it is on the intended line of the putt. Spike mark **2** may look safe but if the putt misses and the ball rolls below the hole, it could be on the intended line of the putt. Spike mark **3** should be safe to repair before the players have holed out. The other two should be left until after holing out.*

other side, and therefore Ogle was wrong to ask for the spike marks to be repaired, and Chapman was wrong to comply. Both men should have been penalized two strokes for a breach of **Rule 13-2**. When the incident came to light later that evening, they had already signed for an incorrect score (one that did not include the two penalty strokes) and so were subsequently disqualified.

Any pitch marks can be repaired, however, and it is good practice to repair a couple on every green if time allows. Of the many sins it is possible to commit on a golf course, failure to replace divots, rake bunkers or repair pitch marks are probably the most prevalent — and the most infuriating for golfers following behind.

Cleaning and replacing balls

George and the captain were both entitled to mark, lift and clean their golf balls when they were on the green **(Rule 16-1b)** — and that means when any part of the ball touches the green. They should use

Above left and right: The correct way to mark your ball so that your marker is off the line of the other player's putt. You may move the marker by two or three putter's head widths away if necessary. But when the player first places his putter on the ground, he must line it up with a fixed object in the distance so that he can replace the marker accurately.

a small coin or a specially made ball marker, which should be pushed into the ground behind the ball. If another ball is on, or near, your line to the hole you should always ask for it to be marked in this way because for your ball to strike another on the green incurs a two-stroke penalty if your ball was played from the putting surface **(Rule 19-5)**.

The captain was furthest from the hole and, as with all golf shots, therefore played first. Having cleaned and replaced

his ball he walked to the hole, lightly brushing away a few leaves with his putter head *(see 'loose impediments', Chapter 6)*. He could also use his hand but would have to be careful to use only enough pressure as was needed to remove the leaves. Testing the surface of a green is against the rules and incurs a two-stroke penalty **(Rule 16-1d)**.

The flagstick

The captain had the choice of having the flagstick removed or attended and asked George to "Tend it, please". George made sure that he did not stand on the line that the captain's ball would take to the hole and checked also that his shadow was not falling on that line. If it was a windy day he would gather in the furls of the flag to stop them flapping noisily around. George also took the precaution of easing the flagstick a little out of the hole to make sure that it would come out freely once the putt had been struck. Any golfer can have the flagstick removed or tended while putting from on the green but if the ball strikes the flagstick a two-stroke addition to the score is the penalty.

George was aware that the flagstick could be left in the hole if he was playing from off the green, and the ball could strike it without penalty, but on the green is a different matter. When the captain struck his putt it rolled straight for the cup but stopped fractionally short and hung agonizingly over the hole. The captain walked up to it and began counting. When he reached 'seven' his ball toppled into the hole and his putt was deemed to have been successful. He explained to George that he is allowed to walk to the hole without reasonable delay and wait for a further 10 seconds to see if the ball will drop **(Rule 16-2)**.

Ball overhanging hole

Sam Torrance fell foul of this rule during the 1990 NM English Open at The Belfry. On the third day, at the 10th green, Sam's ball was overhanging the hole but he was wary of playing it because it was still moving — being rocked by the breeze — and to play a moving ball also incurs a penalty **(Rule 14-5)**. But Sam waited well over the allowed 10 seconds and was consequently penalized one stroke. On the final day he and Mark James birdied the 18th hole to tie for the lead and go into a playoff for the championship. Mark

Right: You may remove loose impediments on the line of your putt with your club (top) or your hand (middle), but you must not use any other equipment or clothing, such as a hat (bottom).

won it on the first extra hole — the 10th, where Sam had been penalized the day before.

It was now George's turn to play and, after surveying his putt from behind his ball, he asked for the flagstick to be removed. The captain did this by laying it on the ground away from the hole in a position where it was in no danger of being hit by George's ball. He did not let it fall from his hand, or throw it violently to the ground as so many amateur golfers do. If the captain was his partner in a competition (rather than his fellow

Right and below: When tending the flagstick stand still with your feet away from the hole. Ensure that the flagstick is loose in the cup and will come away easily. Do not fling the flag away but lay it down gently. If you want to spare your back, lay the flag down using your putter head.

Above: If your ball overhangs the hole, you are allowed to reach the hole without unreasonable delay and a further 10 seconds. If the ball falls in the hole within this time, you are considered to have holed out with your previous stroke.

Above: The player, his partner, or either of their caddies, may point out the line of a putt but they must not touch the putting surface (Rule 8) or they will incur a two-stroke penalty in strokeplay or loss of hole in matchplay.

competitor) or his caddie, George could have asked for advice on the expected line of his putt. When giving such advice, someone may point out the suggested line, using, for example, the base of the flagstick, but must not allow his pointer to touch the ground **(Rule 16-1)**.

When we see pro players taking elaborate and circuitous walks around the putting green it may be because they want to survey the putt from all angles but often it is simply a matter of avoiding someone else's line to the hole. It is probably safer to regard the path between

ball and cup as sacrosanct and inviolable except to:
● Repair pitch marks.
● Remove loose impediments *(see Chapter 6)*.

One final word about the green: although you cannot repair spike marks before putting, once the hole is completed it is a good idea to tamp down any that you see.

Key points

1 Divots on the tee should not be replaced.
2 Pitch marks can, and should, be repaired at any time.
3 Spike marks on the line of your intended putt cannot be repaired.
4 If a ball played from the putting surface hits the flagstick, the player incurs a two-stroke penalty.

The fourth hole

The 4th hole on George's course was a par 5 of 498 yards and intimidating in the extreme, having two large water hazards. A water hazard is any sea, lake, pond, river, ditch, surface draining ditch, or other open water course (**Section II: Definitions**). But it does not have to contain water — indeed, if the weather has been mild and particularly dry without any rain, many are drier than a Manhattan martini. There are two types of water hazard — lateral and ordinary, and it is the latter that can be found on this particular hole. Water hazards are marked by yellow stakes or posts (lateral water hazards by red ones) and anything within the margin of the stakes is considered to be in the hazard. The stakes themselves are also part of the hazard.

Water hazards

The first problem on the hole was a large pond that started 20 yards in front of the tee and continued on for another 120 yards. For most players a carry of that distance would be a routine 6- or 7-iron, but the water usually had the effect on George of making him so nervous that he had difficulty gripping the club, let alone swinging it to good effect.

When it was his turn to play, having watched the captain effortlessly clear the hazard with his tee shot, George, to nobody's surprise, least of all his own, dumped his ball in the middle of the pond. He looked inquiringly at the captain who was, by now, beginning to

Above: A ball may be in a water hazard but completely dry. Remember that your first option in a water hazard is to play the ball as it lies.

enjoy his role as teacher. Most of us like being in a position where we can pass on knowledge to others and the majority of golfers are quite happy to share information on rules and etiquette if asked. It is when other players flagrantly break rules — either through ignorance or wilful stupidity — that experienced golfers get angry.

George asked: "I suppose my ball is lost and I have to play stroke and distance, don't I?"

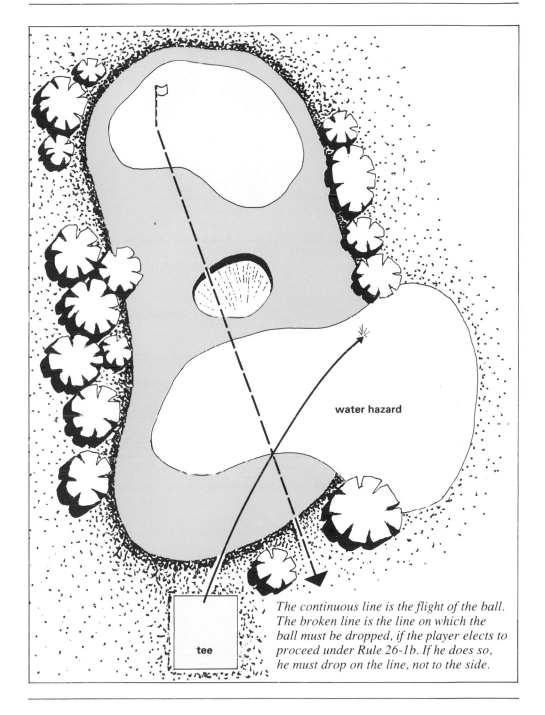

water hazard

tee

The continuous line is the flight of the ball. The broken line is the line on which the ball must be dropped, if the player elects to proceed under Rule 26-1b. If he does so, he must drop on the line, not to the side.

"Not necessarily," replied the captain. "The first thing we have to do is decide whether the ball is lost in the hazard (**Rule 26-1**). I know that may sound silly but it is not uncommon for a ball that you see make a splash to either hit something and bounce back out or to skim along the top of the water. However, in this case we both saw it disappear in the middle of the pond and no evidence has arisen to suggest that it is not gone forever; therefore, we assume it is lost in the water hazard."

This rule has been well learnt no doubt by the American pro golfer Steve Jones. In the 1989 Bell South Classic he struck his ball towards a water hazard, saw it splash and assumed it had gone to a watery grave. Without saying anything he teed up another ball and put it into play. but unseen by him, his original ball had struck something and bounced back out of the water hazard. By not saying: "I will play a provisional ball" he had implicitly declared his first ball lost and was penalized two strokes for illegally putting a second ball in play.

But having established that George's ball was lost in the water hazard, the captain continued: "You therefore have three choices if your ball lies in, touches, or is lost in a water hazard (**Rule 26-1**). The first...." at which point George smilingly interrupted: "is stroke and distance". "Quite right," said the captain, "and the second, also under one-stroke penalty, is that you can drop a ball anywhere you like backwards along a line which keeps the point where your ball entered the hazard between you and the hole."

"You mean," said George, "that it is like one of my options when the ball was unplayable — I could go back as far as I wanted, as long as I kept the point where I found the ball between me and the hole?"

"Yes, it is like that, I suppose," the captain replied. "But instead of keeping the point where you found the ball between you and the hole, in this instance you keep the point where the ball crossed the margin of the hazard between you and the hole. You mark the place where your ball entered the hazard, get that in line with the hole, and go back as far as you want."

"But in this case," said George, "the water hazard is only a few yards in front of the tee, so wouldn't I be better off taking the stroke and distance option, because at least then I can tee the ball up again. If I choose to play from a line behind the pond I will have to drop the ball and it may fall or roll into an awkward spot.

The captain agreed with this assessment so George teed up once more and this time hit a fine shot that carried the pond easily — why is this always so simple the second time around?

But as they were walking towards their drives, George said: "Didn't you mention that I had three choices if my ball was in, touching or lost in a water hazard?"

"I did," said the captain, "and was wondering when you would ask. The third option, and one that many people overlook, is that you can play it as it lies. You often see professional players don their waterproofs and try to play a ball from water. I remember seeing Christy O'Connor Jr attempting to play a shot from the Swilken Burn — the stream that guards the first green at St Andrews — during the 1989 Dunhill Cup. And the American Masters championship has been decided a few times when players elected to play from the streams that guard the 13th and 15th greens. In this

instance that option was not open to you because we both saw your ball disappear in the middle of the pond but often it can be one of your choices.

"You see, to play from a water hazard does not necessarily mean getting wet because the markers defining the hazard are often several feet, or yards, from the water itself. Take this pond, for example. It has a grassy bank leading down to the water but the yellow stakes are at the top of the banking. If your ball came to rest on the grass bank it would be within the margins of the hazard **(Rule 13-4b)**. And a hazard is defined as any water hazard

Above: An option often forgotten by many players is that a ball in a water hazard can be played as it lies. Here, the ball is within the margins of the lateral water hazard but not in the water and can therefore be played with care.

or bunker **(Section II: Definitions)**."

The two players continued on their way to the green and George's anxiety increased with each step. The putting surface was also guarded by water, this time in the form of a wide stream that ran across in front of the green — and George had always experienced trouble in getting over it. The captain had layed up short with his second shot, as had George with his fourth (because he played three off the tee). As he walked to his ball he confided his fear of the shot to the captain who advised George to look not at the water hazard, nor at the flag, but at some point well past the green. To his delighted surprise, George found that this worked and his ball soared satisfyingly high before coming to rest 20 feet from the flag.

But his surprise was doubled when the captain, hitting his worst shot of the round so far, lifted his head a fraction as he struck the ball. In consequence he did not hit it quite clean and, although the ball barely cleared the stream, it then rolled slowly back into the water hazard.

The captain muttered under his breath and, using a long scoop provided by the club, fished his ball out, cleaned it and proceeded to drop, under one-stroke penalty, on a line back down the fairway. but George was uncertain whether he was dropping in the right place and timidly questioned him.

Below: The ball has crossed the margin of the hazard three times, at A, B and C. But it is the point at which it last crossed the margin that concerns the golfer. He can play the ball as it lies; replay the shot under one-stroke penalty (stroke and distance); or, also under one-stroke penalty, drop as far back along the dotted line as he wishes. If he selects the third he must drop on the line, not to the side.

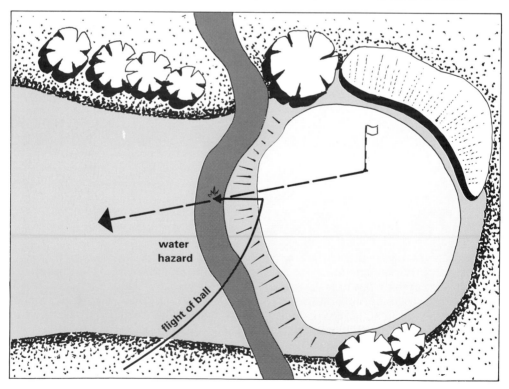

water
hazard

flight of ball

Above: Here the ball is nestling against a stake that defines a water hazard. The stake is part of the hazard so the player is not entitled to relief without penalty.

"I know what you mean," the captain answered, "and this can be a little confusing but, in a situation like this you always use your point of reference as the point where the ball last crossed the margin of the hazard. My ball flew across the stream at an angle, because I was coming in from the right side of the fairway. If it had gone straight in the stream then I would have dropped using the point where it crossed the stream as my mark. But it landed on the far bank and then fell back, so it is where it last crossed the margin of the hazard that I must keep between me and the hole when I am deciding where to drop."

The captain chipped on and two putted, for a total of seven (drive, second layed up, third in the stream, penalty stroke fourth, chip on for five and two putts). George also had seven (three off the tee, fourth layed up, fifth on the green and two putts) and felt secretly pleased that, for the first time, he had not scored worse than his fellow competitor.

Key points

1 Establish that the ball is lost in the water hazard. If you cannot do this with any certainty, proceed under **Rule 27**, which covers the procedure for a lost ball *(see Chapter 1)*.

2 If the ball is in, touching or lost in a water hazard, you may, under one-stroke penalty, play: stroke and distance; or drop the ball on a line that keeps the point where the ball last crossed the margin of the hazard between you and the hole, going as far back as you wish.

3 Without penalty you may play the ball in the hazard, remembering not to ground your club.

4 Water hazards are defined by yellow stakes or lines.

The fifth hole

On the next hole, a relatively short par 4 of 375 yards, the captain still had the honour. As he and George were walking to the tee he invited George to call him by his first name — Edward.

Lateral water hazards

The hole they were about to play was characterized by a lateral water hazard — a ditch that ran all the way to the green, up the right-hand side of the fairway, and the margins of the hazard were marked by red stakes or lines **(Section II: Definitions)**.

The captain played first but, still a little irritated at his uncustomary lapse on the previous hole, half topped the ball so that it moved only about 100 yards. Feeling even more encouraged by these signs of human frailty in a fellow competitor he

Below: A lateral water hazard runs laterally to, or in the same general direction as, the hole. Stakes or lines defining the hazard are in the hazard.

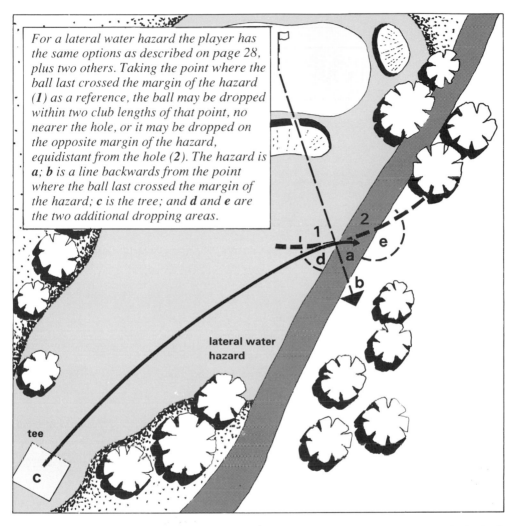

For a lateral water hazard the player has the same options as described on page 28, plus two others. Taking the point where the ball last crossed the margin of the hazard (*1*) as a reference, the ball may be dropped within two club lengths of that point, no nearer the hole, or it may be dropped on the opposite margin of the hazard, equidistant from the hole (*2*). The hazard is *a*; *b* is a line backwards from the point where the ball last crossed the margin of the hazard; *c* is the tree; and *d* and *e* are the two additional dropping areas.

lateral water hazard

tee

had believed invincible, George stepped up with confidence and played his familiar slice. It bounced once on the fairway and jumped into the ditch.

As they proceeded up the fairway, George asked: "Edward, why is it called a lateral water hazard — what distinguishes it from the hazards on the last hole?"

"The name is purely because the hazard runs in a lateral line to the hole," the captain replied, "in the same direction as we play, if you like. As we discussed on the fourth, one of the options if you go into a water hazard is to drop behind the hazard, keeping the point where the ball last entered it between you and the hole. That is still a possibility here but in some cases it is not, because it would be impractical to go backwards. You would

One of the options when seeking relief from a lateral water hazard, under one-stroke penalty, is to drop a ball outside the hazard within two club lengths of the point where the ball last crossed the margin of the hazard, no nearer the hole (Rule 26).

simply be walking along in the hazard and you would find no point of relief.

"To compensate for that you have a further choice, which is, under a one-stroke penalty, to drop within two club lengths, on either side of the hazard (**Rule 26-1c**)."

When they reached the spot where the ball jumped into the ditch, its location was not immediately evident. The ditch had dirty water in the bottom, making a search difficult. But the captain informed George that he was allowed to use a club in this situation to probe under the surface of the water for his ball (**Rule 12-1**). After a couple of minutes he found

Below: The player may go to a point on the opposite margin of the hazard, equidistant from the hole and drop, under one-stroke penalty, within two club lengths of that point.

Opposite top: In this instance the ball rolls back into the hazard from which the player is seeking relief.
Oppposite below: If this happens twice he may place the ball (Rule 20) as near as possible to the spot where it struck the ground when dropped for the second time.

a ball with his club, fished it out and identified it as his.

"So are you clear," the captain asked, "what your options are?"

"I think so," George replied. "As with any water hazard I can play it as it lies — which I have decided here is impractical; I can play stroke and distance; I can go as far back as I wish, keeping the point at which the ball last crossed the margin of the hazard between me and the hole; or I can additionally drop within two club lengths of where the ball last crossed the margin of the hazard between me and the hole; or I can additionally drop within two club lengths of where the ball crossed the margin of the hazard, or within two club lengths of the opposite side of the hazard, equidistant from the hole."

If, however, George, having identified his ball, had decided that he wanted to play it from within the hazard, he would have had to put it back under the water, as near as possible to the lie it had when he found it.

But he sensibly elected to drop within two club lengths and, as he was using his pitching wedge to fish for the ball, and it was still in his hand, he started to measure using this. But the captain pointed out that the Rules do not specifiy which club he must use when measuring two club lengths, and therefore he would be well advised to use the longest in his bag — the driver — in order to gain the maximum possible relief.

He added: "Of course, if you had one of those extra long putters, such as those used by Sam Torrance or Peter Senior, you could technically use that but there is an unwritten code among golfers that this would be against the spirit of the law so I have yet to hear of anyone trying it."

When he had measured off with his driver, George was advised to mark the point two club lengths away from the boundary of the hazard by putting a tee peg in the ground. When he dropped, the ball must land within the two clubs distance but may roll up to another two club lengths away as long as it goes no nearer the hole *(see Chapter 14)*. He played a fair recovery just short of the green, chipped on and two putted, for a total of six strokes (one into the water, penalty drop for two, three short of the green, four chipped on and two putts). The captain chipped and one putted for a par four.

■■■■■ Key points ■■■■■

1 In a lateral water hazard the same options apply as in an ordinary water hazard, with one addition. The ball may be dropped within two club lengths of the point where it last crossed the margin of the hazard, or a point on the other side of the hazard equidistant from the hole, under a one-stroke penalty.
2 Lateral water hazards are defined by red stakes or lines.
3 These stakes or lines are part of the hazard.
4 A ball is in the hazard if any part of it touches the hazard.

The sixth hole

Hole six, George was delighted to remember, was a straightforward 398 yard par 4, with no water hazards and few bunkers. Having watched Edward drive, he hit a good tee shot that landed in the fairway about 10 yards behind the ball of his fellow competitor. He walked off the tee smiling, thinking what a pleasant man Edward had turned out to be and what a wonderful day it was to be out. He should have realized that just as the game of golf begins to look pleasant it will jump up and bite you in the rear.

Obstructions

When they reached his ball he groaned inwardly as he saw that it was sitting on top of a flattened and discarded beer can. The captain cursed loudly at the thought that ill-mannered louts had dared to litter the course in this way. George cursed to himself and said: "Well, I'm bound to have to pay a penalty for this, what is it and how should I proceed?"

"Oh no," answered the captain, "you're quite all right. This a movable obstruction. An obstruction is defined as anything artificial, including the artificial surfaces and sides of roads and paths, except: objects that define out-of-bounds; any part of an immovable artificial object which is out-of-bounds; and any construction declared by the committee to be an integral part of the course."

Probably the best known example of this latter exception is the road at the back of the 17th green of the Old Course at St Andrews — so well known is it that the 17th is called 'The Road Hole'. It has been declared an integral part of the course so golfers have to play off it, or declare their ball unplayable and take relief under penalty. The road, and the hole, are such an idiosyncratic but historical part of the course that no golfers seem to object, particularly as it is so close to the green that they are likely to be playing off it with a putter or pitching wedge.

Less well known is the public footpath that crosses the 18th fairway, about a 9-iron short of the green and which is certainly in driving range when the wind is against. During the 1990 Open Championship at St Andrews the American Payne Stewart, who eventually finished joint second behind Nick Faldo,

Opposite inset: The player's ball has come to rest on an obstruction so he can take relief without penalty. This must be done by finding the point nearest the ball (without crossing over, under or through the obstruction) which is not nearer the hole, avoids interference and is not in a hazard or on a green. In this situation, check the scorecard to ensure the path or road has not been designated an integral part of the course under a local rule. Opposite above: At first glance the nearest point of relief is to the right of the path but, as with casual water in a bunker, the player is entitled to relief for his stance. Opposite below: Once again, the nearest point of relief is to the left.

took exception to this path being considered an integral part of the course. He asked the Royal and Ancient, the organization that stages the Open, who would be responsible if, in the process of playing a full iron shot from a hard tarmacadam surface, he damaged his wrists or hands to the extent that he could not play golf again. The R&A's response has not been recorded.

"If the obstruction interferes with your stance or intended line of swing," the captain continued, "and the ball is not lying in any type of water hazard, you may take relief — that is, drop away from the obstruction, within one club length. You must find the nearest point which is not nearer the hole, avoids interference and would not require you to drop in a hazard or on a putting green. But you must not cross over, through or under the obstruction unless it is the artificial sides and surfaces of a road or path. One other point to bear in mind is that you are not allowed relief just because an obstruction is in your way, between you and the green. It has to be interfering with your stance or intended line of swing."

"But that's no help," said George, who was beginning to get confused by this explanation. "My ball is not affected by an immovable obstruction, it's lying on a tin can."

The captain replied, a little testily, "If you would let me finish, I was just getting round to movable obstructions, of which that can is one. Quite simply, a movable obstruction is also a man-made, artificial object but, as the name suggests, it can be moved. That covers things like benches that aren't bolted to the ground, cigarette packets, litter and wrappers and, essentially, anything that is not part of nature and should not be on the course."

He went on to explain that a movable obstruction can always be moved if it interferes with a player's stance or intended line of swing, and on the green if it is on the line of his putt. If the ball is not lying in or on the object, the object can simply be stowed in the golf bag, to be discarded later or, in the case of a

Below: You are allowed to move loose impediments (natural objects such as leaves) at any time as long as they and the ball do not lie in or touch a hazard (Rule 23). But if a ball, through the green, moves while you are removing a loose impediment within a club's length of the ball, there is a one-stroke penalty (Rule 18). On the green, there is no penalty and the ball should be replaced.

bench, for example, moved temporarily out of the way. If the ball moves during this procedure, the ball should be replaced without penalty.

In George's case, because his ball was lying on the can, it could be lifted and cleaned, the can removed and then the ball dropped, as near as possible to where it lay before the can was taken away but not nearer the hole.

"Let me just see if I've got this straight," said George, "An obstruction is an artificial or man-made object. If it interferes with my stance or intended line of stroke I can drop away from it if it is immovable, and get rid of it if it is movable, without penalty."

"Yes. Essentially you should look on them as things that should not be there, in which case it is wrong for you to be penalized if they interfere with your shot."

Loose impediments

Feeling mightily relieved, George lifted and cleaned his ball, stowed the can in his golf bag, dropped the ball as near as possible to where it had lain on the can and played his second shot. It was well hit but just missed the green on the right.

Below: If the ball moves while you are removing a loose impediment, through the green, you incur a one-stroke penalty (Rule 18) and the ball must be replaced.

When he reached it, George discovered that this time his ball had nestled against a fallen tree branch and he was about to pull the branch away when the captain stopped him with a shout.

"You can't dop that, I'm afraid. You have to play the ball as it lies or declare it unplayable."

"But there's a great big branch up against it," George spluttered. "That's not fair."

"What you have to remember," the captain explained, "is that nothing in golf is meant to be fair. If your ball hits a stone and kicks out-of-bounds, or gets stuck in a tree, you just have to accept it. That branch is not man-made or artificial and is not, therefore, classified as an obstruction, movable or otherwise. It is a part of nature, a natural object and is therefore a loose impediment. These include worms and insects and casts made by them, stones, leaves, branches and so on. But an important exception is a bird's nest which, although technically a loose impediment because it is natural, has been defined as a movable obstruction in order to protect the birds."

"So you're telling me that I can't remove a loose impediment?" George asked.

"Not at all," the captain answered. "A loose impediment can be removed at any time except when you are in a hazard. But if your ball moves while you're doing so, you incur a penalty stroke. And if you move a loose impediment that is within a club length of your ball, without actually touching the ball, and the ball moves, you are 'deemed' to have caused its movement and are still penalized (**Rule 18-2c**)."

Muttering to himself, George decided that the only course open to him was to declare his ball unplayable and take a penalty drop, which he did, within two club lengths. He chipped on and holed a good putt for a five (one off the tee, two to the branch, the third was a penalty drop, fourth onto the green and one putt). The captain made a rock solid par.

▬▬▬▬ Key points ▬▬▬▬

1 Obstructions are artificial, man-made objects.

2 If an immovable obstruction interferes with his stance or intended line of swing anywhere on the course, a player may take relief, within one club length, without penalty.

3 If a movable obstruction interferes with his stance or intended line of swing anywhere on the course, a player may dispose of the obstruction without penalty.

4 A loose impediment is a natural object that can be moved at any time outside a hazard, provided that the ball does not move as well.

5 A bird's nest is a movable obstruction, not a loose impediment.

6 If a player removes a loose impediment within one club length of his ball, and the ball moves, irrespective of whether he touched it, he is deemed to have caused it to move and penalized one stroke.

The seventh hole

Still chafing at the unfairness of life in general and golf in particular, George arrived on the tee of the 7th hole, a 410 yard par 4. When it was his turn to play he hit his best drive of the day, probably because he was still thinking about loose impediments and not trying to remember to keep his left arm straight, hold his head still, coil fully on the backswing and carry on to a high finish. Suddenly, life looked good again. In contrast, the captain had hit a little behind the ball and progressed it only about 100 yards towards the green.

Casual water

This rare display of ineptitude surprised George but the lie of the captain's ball surprised him even more. It sat in the middle of a large but shallow puddle of accumulated water in the middle of the fairway. Because water is natural and the puddle was a product of nature, George assumed that, like his earlier lie against a loose impediment, the captain would just have to accept his unfortunate situation or take a penalty drop. But the captain merely waded into the puddle, picked up his ball and waded out again.

He saw George studying him a little quizically and explained: "This is what is known as casual water and I get a free drop. Casual water is any temporary accumulation of water that is visible before or after the player takes his stance and is not in a water hazard. It can include overflow from a water hazard as long as it is outside the margins of the

hazard. Dew is not casual water whereas snow and ice can be either casual water or a loose impediment. The player must decide for himself **(Rule 25 Definitions)**."

The exception to this is manufactured ice, which is an obstruction — presumably a movable one. So if your ball nestles up against a lump of ice caused by overnight frost, you can regard it as casual water or a loose impediment. If the ice has just been discarded by a fellow golfer who is in the habit of carrying an iced drink with him when he plays, it is an obstruction. In truth, it matters little how you define it; in the former case you can drop away from casual water or move the loose impediment (making sure not to move the ball), and in the latter you can move the obstruction, replacing your ball if it also moves, in either case without penalty.

The captain said: "If my ball lies in or touches casual water, or the water interferes with my stance or intended line of swing, I can take relief at the point nearest where the ball lies which avoids the water, that is not nearer the hole and not in a hazard or on a green. I lift the ball and, having lifted it, can clean it if I wish, and can drop within one club's length of the spot which fulfills all these conditions. As you can see, I am standing within a club's length of the edge of the puddle, am not nearer the hole and am not about to drop into a hazard or onto a green. Therefore my drop here would be legal. Once it hits the ground the ball is allowed to roll up to two club lengths

Above: A player may take relief without penalty from a hole, cast or runway made by a burrowing animal, a reptile or bird if his ball is in or touches the condition, He may also take relief if his stance or the intended line of his swing are afffected. Through the green he finds the nearest point of relief, lifts and drops within one club length, no nearer the hole, avoiding interference by the condition and not in a hazard or on a green.

Opposite top and below: A player may play a ball as it lies in ground under repair (Rule 25) although this is often prohibited by a local rule. But as with casual water, holes, casts or runways made by burrowing animals, reptiles and birds, he may also take relief. Here he has dropped the ball clear but his stance is still affected by the GUR. Therefore he should drop again, without penalty, within one club length of the nearest point of relief, no nearer the hole, not in a hazard or on a green and avoiding the condition.

away, no nearer the hole. If it rolls back into the casual water I can drop it again **(Rule 20-2)**.

"As it happens I am lucky because I am dropping on the fairway. If the nearest point of relief happened to be in a bush, in the rough or in any other unhelpful place, so be it — I would just have to bite the bullet and get on with it, or decide to

play from the casual water after all. But conversely, if my ball was in the rough and the nearest point of relief was on the fairway, that is where I would drop."

Many golfers get confused about this and assume that a drop without a penalty

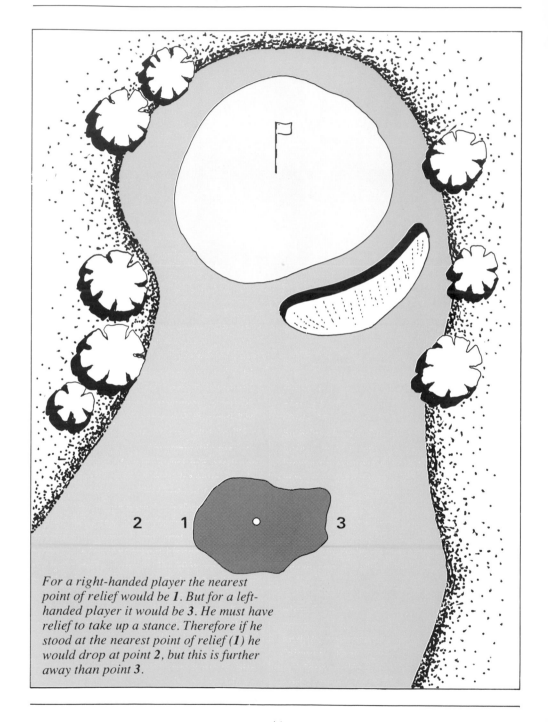

For a right-handed player the nearest point of relief would be **1**. But for a left-handed player it would be **3**. He must have relief to take up a stance. Therefore if he stood at the nearest point of relief (**1**) he would drop at point **2**, but this is further away than point **3**.

entitles them to drop in a favourable place. Not so. The nearest point of relief is exactly that, not the nearest point of relief that gives the player a good position. Should the casual water be on the green, the player may lift and replace the ball in the nearest spot that offers relief and he can do this whether his stance and intended line of swing are affected, or whether the intended line of the putt is affected. The ball itself may not be in casual water on the green but the path to the hole may have casual water on it. In such a case the player may move his ball so that he faces a putt that does not have to negotiate a puddle on its way to the cup, as long as he does not move the ball nearer the hole.

Unusual ground conditions

On the captain's next shot he faced a similar problem but this time his ball had come to rest in a rabbit scrape. Once again he took relief, without penalty.

He told George: "The Rules allow relief from ground under repair (GUR) or a hole, cast or runway made by a burrowing animal, reptile or bird **(Rule 25)**. The circumstances are exactly the same as for casual water. The exception is water hazards of any kind. It is impossible to find casual water in a water hazard and there is no relief either from GUR or the holes, scrapes or other conditions made by birds, reptiles or burrowing animals **Rule 25-1b)**".

Ground under repair is exactly what it sounds like and is increasingly common on parched fairways that are becoming denuded of grass. It can be marked by stakes but is usually defined by a white line. A golf club committee can make a local rule prohibiting play from GUR and usually does. If the ball lies in a bunker, it must be dropped within the bunker and if it rolls out it must be dropped again. If it rolls out once more it must be placed. The player is allowed to seek the maximum available relief from the condition but is not entitled to complete relief. But he does have one further option in a bunker. He can drop outside the hazard, keeping the point where the ball lay between him and the hole, but he exercises this option at the cost of a penalty stroke **(Rule 25-1 (b)ii)**.

The captain, possibly realizing that he had been fortunate in comparison to George's tribulations on previous holes, took his drop but fluffed the shot, took another onto the green and proceeded to three putt for the first time that day, taking a total of seven strokes. Meanwhile, George had found the green with his second shot and recorded his first par of the day.

■■■■ Key points ■■■■

1 A player can obtain relief, without penalty, from casual water, ground under repair and 'certain damage' to the course.
2 If the ball is in a bunker it must be dropped in the bunker.
3 Through the green, relief must be taken at the nearest point allowed under the Rules, irrespective of where that might be.
4 The player is allowed maximum available relief in a bunker — not complete relief.
5 From a bunker (but not a water hazard) he may also drop out, under a one-stroke penalty, keeping the point where the ball lay between him and the hole.

The eighth hole

The 8th hole, a 180 yard par 3, was one of George's favourites. The green nestled in a copse of bushes and the approach was lined with trees and had many different sorts of flowering shrubs. But he was also fond of it, it has to be said, because it was a hole he invariably played well and the two things usually go together.

Glowing with the pride of having taken the honour he stepped briskly onto the tee with his 5-wood, a club that he knew was the right one for him on this hole. He teed his ball up and, as he swung back, just at the top of his backswing, the quiet of the course was shattered by a shriek of delight from an adjoining green. George nearly dropped his club but luckily, he had not started a forward movement with the intention of hitting the ball so he was not considered to have made a stroke **(Rule 14 Definitions)**. Nor would he have made a stroke if he had stopped his downswing before the club reached the ball.

Golf etiquette

Loud laughter and chatter carried clearly from the nearby 17th green, where one of a fourball had obviously holed an important putt to win the match and the money from his playing partners. George was irritated but prepared to resume his stance when he noticed the captain marching off to the 17th green. After exchanging a few brief words with the fourball they fell silent and quietly moved to the 18th tee as the captain strode purposefully back.

"Good heavens, Edward, whatever did you say?" George asked him.

The captain replied, "This is not a football field and although someone is entitled to be pleased if he makes a good shot, he is not entitled to disturb everyone else on the course. Mind you," he added with a twinkle, "being captain does have its privileges and once I said who I was and reminded them where they were they soon shut up."

George re-addressed his ball and swung. There was a satisfying click from his clubface and the ball soared high, suspended for a moment against a startlingly blue backdrop before falling to earth. George knew it was a good shot the moment he hit it and had those few precious seconds of wondering just how good before it surpassed even his expectations by pitching on the front of the green, taking two hops and rolling straight in the hole. A hole-in-one — an ace!

For a moment he was too overwhelmed to speak or to believe what his eyes had just told him but he was brought back to earth by a resounding slap on the back from the captain, a firm handshake and the words: "Well done, George, well done". George smiled broadly and felt an overpowering urge to break into a loud holler but, remembering the captain's admonition of the fourball on the 17th, he refrained.

After the captain had played, George asked Edward: "Edward, why were you so firm with that group on the 17th? They weren't being malicious, they just got a little carried away."

"I know, George, perhaps I was a little hasty but they should have consideration for others. The Rules of Golf are almost entirely drawn up of definitions, penalties and descriptions but they do have their priorities right — the section on etiquette comes right at the beginning, and so it should."

George was a little surprised to hear this and asked what Section I of the Rules says.

"In essence," said the captain, "it says we should have consideration of others at heart, be mindful of their safety, and take good care of the course. Obviously safety is important so you do not stand near

Above: Bunkers should always be raked when you leave them, and thoroughly enough that no players coming behind should know you were in the sand.

someone about to make a practice swing or, conversely, make a practice swing yourself if people are standing nearby.

"Consideration for others is the sort of thing we have been doing on the way round and, although you admit to knowing very little about the Rules, you have, probably unconsciously, absorbed a great deal about etiquette. When it is my turn to play, for example, you do not chatter, fidget from foot to foot, stand too close or jingle coins in your pocket; neither do you stand directly behind the ball or on the other side of the hole if I am putting.

"You know never to strike a shot if the

group in front is still in range and that we ourselves should move briskly, particularly when it is time to leave the green. It is infuriating to be standing in the fairway waiting to play while the group ahead stand around the hole trying to work out their score, or they park their trolleys on the wrong side of the green and we have to wait while they fetch them, but we are all guilty of forgetfulness at times. It is one of those strange ironies of golf that the match ahead always seems to be made up of slow golfers who take forever to do anything, while the match behind is always comprised of a group of youngsters who haven't got any patience.

"But a couple of specifics you should bear in mind, because a lot of people do not, is that a two-ball match, like us today, should have precedence over three-or four-ball matches and be entitled to pass them — unless, of course, there is a local rule to the contrary. Many people do not realize that this principle is established in the Rules, and is not just a tradition.

"Another point to bear in mind is that the ball furthest from the hole shall be played first **(Rule 10-1b)**. Most people know this but it is one of the few areas where the professional players do not give us a clear lead; they can often be seen standing at their own ball, in front of their fellow competitors, before the other chap has played. It is easy to see why

Below and opposite: Divots must always be replaced and firmly stamped down. A divot replaced quickly stands a good chance of taking root but if left for twenty four hours it will die.

because with all their yardage charts and preparation it would hold up play interminably if they didn't. Also, they are rightly confident of each other's abilities and know that standing ahead of another professional holds little risk. But for us it's another matter and you should never stand ahead of another player while he is making his stroke, even if you are several yards over to the side. This isn't incorporated in the Rules but it is common sense and courtesy.''

As they reached the green the captain reminded George that the Rules' section on ctiquette also expects players to rake bunkers, replace divots (but not on the tee), repair pitch marks, repair spike marks (but only after the hole has been completed) and generally be careful on the green. For example, they should not lean on their putters, which can be potentially damaging to the greens. One final word about the grccn concerns handling the flagstick. It should be laid aside, not flung away as if in pique.

When they reached the green George lovingly retrieved his ball from the hole and put it in his golf bag, as a souvenir. The captain was short of the green and chipped on and two putted for a four.

Key points

1 Etiquette is common sense. Treat others with consideration and respect.
2 Repair any damage to the course that it is reasonable for you to do.

The ninth hole

The 9th hole was a 498 yard par 5, which normally filled George with trepidation for its sheer length rather than any inherent difficulty it contained. But today, glowing with the pride that only a hole-in-one can bring, he radiated confidence from the tee. Surprisingly under the circumstances, he hit a fine drive, as did the captain.

They walked in amiable silence towards their drives, happily lost in their own pleasant thoughts on golf. For his second shot George faced a dilemma because about 170 yards in front of him was a cross bunker the width of the fairway. Usually this did not come into play for his second shot, but after a fine drive he now had to decide whether to attempt to carry the beast or lay up short. Still flushed with success and consequently not thinking very clearly, he took out a 5-wood and whaled away at the ball in

Below: If a ball in a hazard is covered by loose impediments or sand, the player may remove enough to enable him to see that a ball is there (Rule 12). If too much is removed, it must be replaced, but without

penalty. If the ball is moved during the process, it shall be replaced, also without penalty. The player does not have to identify it as his – no penalty is incurred for playing the wrong ball from a hazard.

sublime but misplaced confidence. This was quickly replaced by hard-nosed reality as his ball, as a result of a topped shot, rolled unerringly into the sand. The captain hit a 6-iron to lay up comfortably short and then put his third into a bunker to the right of the green.

Hazards

When they reached the fairway bunker into which George's ball had disappeared, it was to discover that, because of autumn leaves, the ball was not immediately visible. "Oh no!," George exclaimed. "I suppose that's lost, is it? I know I can't move loose impediments in a hazard so

Above: In a hazard, whether it is a bunker or a water hazard, you must not ground your club or touch the water with it (Rule 13) unless specifically permitted by the Rules, such as when probing for a lost ball.

looking for the ball could be a bit of a problem.''

"No, you're OK," the captain replied. "In a hazard, if the ball is covered by loose impediments, which these leaves clearly are, you are entitled to remove as much as necessary to allow you to see a part of the ball **(Rule 12-1)**. If we thought the ball was covered by sand we could also remove enough sand to similarly identify a ball. What we have to

remember though, is that nothing entitles you to see all of your ball when playing a stroke. All you can do is move enough material to be able to say that a ball is there.

"In fact, there are three things you are normally not allowed to do in a hazard **(Rule 13-4)**. You cannot 'test the condition' in that hazard or a similar one. That means you cannot, for example, feel with your hand to find out if the sand is coarse or fine, wet or dry. You also cannot go to another hazard to test that. In practice, of course, you need to do neither because when you settle your feet in the sand that should tell you everything you need to know. The second thing you cannot do is touch the ground in a hazard with a club. Thirdly, you cannot touch or move a loose impediment that is lying in or touching the hazard; except, of course, in a situation like this when you need to find your ball **(Rule 12-1)**.

Both men proceeded to search, brushing aside the leaves, when George

Above: If two balls lie close to each other in a bunker, the one nearest the hole may be marked and lifted while the other is played.

Opposite top: Because playing the first ball is likely to alter the lie of the second considerably, the ball to be lifted should be marked away from where it lies – a club's length should be sufficient.

Opposite below: But when the ball is lifted the player should make a careful note of its lie because he will need to recreate it as near as possible before replacing, not dropping, his ball.

suddenly groaned and said: "Oh no! I've just moved my ball; that must mean that I've incurred a penalty."

Ball moved in a hazard

"Actually it doesn't," the captain replied. "This is one of those examples where the rule makers have taken the very reasonable assumption that if you cannot

see the ball it would be unfair to penalize you for moving it. What you must do, however, is replace the ball and replace the loose impediments that were covering it, just leaving enough of the ball visible for you to play it. And if the position of the leaves means that you can see the ball from the side, but not when you stand over and address it, that is hard luck. You are not entitled to be able to see it when you play **(Rule 12-1)**."

George played a fine recovery shot that came up just short of the green. However, when he reached the ball and prepared to hit his fourth shot he looked down and said: "Hang on a minute, this isn't mine. I must have played the wrong ball from the bunker — now that must mean that I incur a penalty, doesn't it, Edward?"

Once again the captain smiled: "Wrong again, George. You can relax. Yet again the R&A has decided that if you can only see a small amount of the ball you should not be penalized for playing the wrong one because you were not in a position to identify it properly. You have gained yourself a golf ball, to partly compensate for your earlier losses, and now we must resume the search in the bunker for your original ball."

This they did. Having spent two minutes looking earlier, they knew that they had another three minutes in which to search, and they found George's original ball within that time. Being mindful of the time they had taken and anxious to get on with the hole, George played hastily and saw his shot fly straight into the same greenside bunker into which the captain had gone earlier.

Balls together in a hazard

When they reached the hazard it was to discover that both balls were nestling side by side, with George's being fractionally closer to the hole. He said nothing but looked questioningly at the captain.

"Well, George," Edward asked him, "what would you think the ruling was in this situation?"

"I would think it is you to play first," George answered, "but it is obvious that if you attempt a shot as the balls lie now, mine will be moved. It therefore seems obvious that I will have to mark my ball and move it until after you have played your shot. However, because you will probably make a big hole in the sand, I'm not quite sure how we would go about doing that."

"Absolutely right, so what we do is mark as near as possible to your ball, and using a tee peg would probably be better than a coin. But we must have a good look at the way your ball is lying because after I have played we must try to reproduce your original lie as much as possible **(Rule 20-3b)**."

Both men eventually played out of the bunker without further incident and two putted for bogey sixes.

■■■■■■ Key points ■■■■■■

1 In a bunker a player may move enough sand or loose impediments as necessary to find a ball.
2 He is not necessarily entitled to see the ball when making a stroke.
3 There is no penalty for playing a wrong ball from a hazard.
4 If two balls lie side by side in a hazard, one must be marked and before it is played its lie should, as near as possible, be re-created.

The tenth hole

George was relieved to get the bunkers behind him, or so he thought. As he teed up on the 410 yard par 4 10th he little realized that his acquaintanceship with sand was about to be renewed.

Bunkers

He and Edward played without incident to the fairway but, whereas the captain's approach shot found the green, George once again visited a greenside bunker. However, when he reached the sand it was to discover that his ball was not embedded in it but sitting on a grass island in the centre and a small tree branch was immediately behind it.

"Oh blast, there's a loose impediment interfering with the line of my intended stroke but as I am in a bunker there's nothing I can do about it," he said.

"As a matter of fact, there is," the captain replied, "because that grass is not part of the bunker. A bunker is defined as a prepared area of ground, often a hollow, from which turf or soil has been removed and replaced with sand or the like. Grass covered ground bordering or within a bunker is not part of the bunker **(Section II: Definitions)**. You can therefore treat the loose impediment as you

Below: A grass island within a bunker is not part of the bunker. The player may therefore ground his club while addressing the ball.

would if it were anywhere else through the green, which means that you can remove it as long as, in so doing, you do not move your ball.''

George, who was beginning to find that bunkers are not the horrible places he once thought they were, and that he got a lot more licence under the Rules in hazards than he had previously believed, removed the branch and played his shot. But his sense of relief was quickly followed by disbelief as he lifted his head too quickly, thinned the shot and sent it flying at knee height across the green straight into another bunker. He carefully raked the bunker, as he knew he must, before trudging wearily across the green to play his fourth shot.

This time his ball was nestling against a cigar butt — which he knew he could remove because it is a movable obstruction, taking care to replace his ball if it should move in the process — but it also had a stone immediately behind it. The stone was, of course, a loose impediment and George was cursing his bad luck when

Above: If the player brushes the sand in a bunker with the club during his backswing, he incurs two penalty strokes for grounding his club in a hazard.

the captain said: ''Don't worry, George. You can take it away because a local rule allows us to remove stones from bunkers without penalty.''

To prove the point he showed George the back of his scorecard where the local rules were enshrined. Of course, George did not reveal that he had no idea that the card contained so much useful information. Instead, he took up his stance, being careful not to touch the sand with his club, but as he took the club back it brushed the top of the sand. George appeared not to notice and continued with his execution of the shot but he hit a poor recovery that thumped into the front of the bunker and rolled back to his feet. He moved quickly so that the ball would not touch him and watched in despair as it settled into one of his footprints.

Grounding the club

"Oh no!" said George, as he banged the head of his club into the sand. "Look at the rotten lie I've got now."

"I'm afraid it's even worse than that," commented the captain, "because you've also incurred four penalty strokes." As George spluttered and choked the captain explained: "I'm not sure if you noticed but as you took the clubhead back it brushed the sand so you have incurred two penalty strokes for breach of **Rule 13-4** — touching the ground in a hazard with your club. But then in your anger you banged the club into the sand, incurring a further two penalty strokes for repeating the offence."

George looked horrified and, as he stared at the captain in disbelief, his club slipped from his numb fingers and fell into the sand. He groaned loudly and said: "And there's another two penalty strokes for good measure."

"No, George, if you accidentally drop a club, or lose your footing and put your hand in the bunker to stop falling, or drop the rake in the bunker to save time when you have played your shot, none of them constitutes an offence as long as nothing is done that improves the lie of your ball **(1990 Decisions)**. But, of course, had you moved the ball, you would have been subject to a further penalty of one stroke **(Rule 18-2)**."

Casual water in a bunker

Anxious to get out of the bunker as quickly as possible, George took a huge swipe and again thinned it across the green into a third bunker. After again raking the sand smooth he walked disconsolately around the ground to find

that the bunker was full of water and his ball was nowhere to be seen. Seeing his dejection the captain trawled the rake through the water and removed George's ball.

"OK, Edward, what do I do now," asked George.

"It's actually quite straightforward, even though you have four options. Your ball was lying in casual water so you are allowed a drop without penalty but, as it was a hazard, it has to be dropped within the hazard. Now I know that the bunker is filled with water but that is hard luck — you are entitled to the maximum available relief, not complete relief, therefore you have to drop in the water where it is shallowest. You could, of course, have played it where it lay but because we couldn't even see it; that was never really an option. Your third choice is to drop the ball behind the bunker, as far back as you like, keeping the point where we found the ball between you and the hole **(Rule 25-1b)**. Finally, you could declare the ball unplayable and proceed under **Rule 28**, and you know that your options there are stroke and distance; take a drop within two club lengths but not nearer the hole; and go back on a line as far as you want. But if you accept either of these last two options you must drop the ball in the bunker."

"But we've already established that that wouldn't do me any good at all," George said.

"Exactly," replied the captain. "So really your choices are to drop at the point of nearest available relief in the bunker or go back outside the bunker, under a one stroke penalty."

George reluctantly took this last option, chipped on to the green but, with his concentration completely shot, three putted for a sickening total of fourteen

Opposite top: A ball in casual water in a bunker may be lifted and dropped, without penalty as near as possible to where it lay but not nearer the hole, in ground that offers maximum available relief (Rule 25). At first glance, it appears that the nearest point of relief is to the right of the water. Opposite below: But the player can take relief for interference to his stance. If he stood clear of the water, he would drop the ball several feet further away than the water's edge.

Above: If he goes to the left of the casual water his stance is clear and he can now drop at the nearest point of maximum available relief

strokes (his second found the grassy bank in the first bunker, the third across the green into the second bunker, the fourth failed to get out and rolled back into his footprint, four penalty strokes were added for touching the sand twice, the ninth went into the water-filled bunker, the tenth was a penalty drop behind that bunker, the eleventh found the green and there were three putts). The captain two putted for a par four.

■■■ Key points ■■■

1 Always rake a bunker when you leave it.
2 Areas of grass, or bushes and the like, within a bunker are not part of the bunker.
3 Local rules often allow stones to be removed from a bunker without penalty.
4 You are not permitted to ground a club deliberately in a bunker or any hazard.
5 From casual water in a bunker you are allowed the maximum available relief, not complete relief.
6 You may declare your ball unplayable at any time unless the ball lies in or touches a water hazard.

The eleventh hole

Still reeling from the shock of taking fourteen strokes, George was deep in his own thoughts as the captain stepped on to the 11th tee, the starting point of a 392 yard par 4. The captain, possibly also a little bemused by George's efforts, hit his worst shot of the day, a towering slice into the right-hand rough.

"Did you see where it went?" he asked, to which George was obliged to say: "Oh, I'm sorry, I didn't. I was so wrapped up in my own problems that I didn't even realize you were about to play."

The captain was too polite to reprimand him but George realized his mistake and knew that it is accepted courtesy for all golfers in a group to watch the ball of their opponents or fellow competitors. Not only does it help pinpoint a ball that may be lost but on a sunny day, when it can be difficult to follow the flight of a ball, it greatly helps a player to keep his head still through the shot if he knows that his fellow competitors are spotting his ball for him.

After playing, and finding the fairway, George again apologised but was told by the captain to forget it. "Under the circumstances, I would probably have been miles away myself. I'm going to play a provisional ball and then we can go and

Above: A player may touch or bend long grass, rushes, heather and so on to the extent necessary to find his ball (Rule 12). If the ball moves while he is doing this, he incurs a penalty stroke and must replace the ball.

Opposite: Once the ball is found, the player must be able to identify it as his. If he cannot, his original ball is deemed lost and he must take a stroke and distance penalty.

try to find the other blighter which is, incidentally, an Ultra 4.''

Lost ball

When they reached the rough they proceeded to search and George asked: ''Is there any limit to what we can do in searching for a ball. Can I part the grass with my clubhead, for example?''

''Yes, you can,'' the captain replied, ''and because we are looking for my ball that is a safe option because if you should accidentally move it, we simply replace it but if I, my partner, either of our caddies, our equipment or clothing were to move it then I would incur a penalty stroke **(Rule 18-2)**.

''According to **Rule 12-1**, I am allowed to touch or bend long grass, rushes, bushes, gorse, heather or the like, but only to the extent necessary to find and identify my ball, as long as this does not improve the lie of the ball, the area of my intended swing or my line of play. And, as you now know, if it were in a hazard I would also be able to move as much sand or loose impediments as necessary to help find the ball.

''The other thing to remember, through the green, is that if the ball is in casual water, ground under repair or a hole, cast or runway made by a burrowing animal, reptile or bird, and I accidentally move it, there is no penalty and I replace the ball, unless I am to take relief under **Rule 25-1b** *(see Chapter 15)*.''

After a few more minutes the captain said: ''Hang on, George, there's a ball under this bush. Would you come over while I try to see if it's mine.'' The captain leaned under the bush, marked the spot where his ball lay with a tee peg and brought the ball out. ''There you are,

Above: It may be necessary to mark the ball in order to lift it for identification. When lifted the ball may be cleaned to the extent necessary to identify it.

George, it's my Ultra.''

''Yes, I can see that,'' George replied, ''but why did you want me over here? Surely you can identify it on your own.''

Identifying a ball

''Yes, I can,'' the captain answered, ''but according to **Rule 12-2** I have to give you the opportunity of observing the way I lift and replace the ball, just so there can be no suggestion of hanky-panky. You must also remember that you cannot lift a ball to identify it when you are in a hazard — but remember that you don't receive a penalty for playing the wrong ball out of a hazard so it doesn't really matter.''

Above: The player must tell his opponent, fellow competitor or marker of his intention to lift the ball for identification so that the procedure may be observed if desired. If a player lifts the ball without telling his opponent, fellow competitor or marker or giving them an opportunity to observe, he is penalized one stroke.

Taking up a stance

The captain replaced his ball and proceeded to manoeuvre himself into position to hit it. He was allowed, of course, to move any loose impediments but he was not permitted to break off branches, stamp on the ground behind the ball, plait branches together or stand on them in order to improve the lie of his ball, his intended line of swing or his line of play. In short, if by taking up his stance his body gets in the way of branches or the like, there is no problem. What he cannot do is deliberately hold or force them out of the way. Unfortunately, because he was obliged to stand in an awkward position, the captain hit a poor shot which travelled only 40 yards before disappearing into long grass.

The two players walked ahead to begin another search and, as they were looking, the captain muttered and said: "I think I've just stood on my ball." Sure enough, when they investigated more closely, it became clear that the captain had flattened his ball into the ground.

"Bad luck, Edward," commiserated George and, while he meant it and was genuinely sympathetic, he could not help

but quietly rejoice that it was his ball, for once, that was nestling contentedly on the fairway. "So what happens now?" he asked.

Moving a ball in play

"That, I'm afraid is depressingly easy," the captain said. "I incur a penalty stroke because I have moved a ball in play, and pushing it into the ground like that does constitute moving it **(Rule 18-2a)**. I must now, under **Rule 20-3b**, place the ball in the nearest similar lie to the original lie, not more than one club length away and not nearer the hole or in a hazard. In fact, right next to the indentation mark here fulfils all those criteria."

The captain eventually hacked out to the fairway and took a further four strokes to get down, for a total of eight (one under the bush, two into the long grass, three, a penalty stroke, four onto the fairway and four more). George surpassed his own expectations by making a par four.

Above: If your opponent, fellow competitor or their caddies stand on the ball during a search, you may replace it without penalty (Rule 18). But if you, your partner or your caddies do the same, you must replace it but under a one-stroke penalty.

■■■■ Key points ■■■■

1 Always watch other players' shots.

2 You cannot improve the lie of your ball, intended line of swing or line of shot, except under the Rules.

3 Through the green, if you are lifting a ball to identify it, you must inform your opponent or fellow competitor so that the procedure can be observed if wished.

4 Through the green, if you move your own ball while searching, you incur a penalty stroke and must replace the ball.

The twelfth hole

George stepped on to the 12th tee in silence, knowing enough about golf not to attempt commiserating with Edward. The prospect facing him was a 480 yard par 5 from an elevated tee, the sort of shot to breed confidence in any golfer's heart. But as George was getting ready to play, before he could make his first shot, the ball fell off the tee as he was addressing it.

Ball not in play on the teeing ground

Whenever this had happened before, one of George's golfing partners had always said: "One." It was the same player who said it each time, and George was already beginning to appreciate that the oldest joke in golf (if joke is the proper word), would probably continue to be spoken for as long as the game was played. He knew, of course, that he had not incurred a penalty but waited until after he and Edward had played their drives before asking why.

The captain, eager for a chance to take his mind off the previous hole, explained: "It's quite easy really. Until you make a stroke at the ball on the tee it isn't in play

Right and above right: If a ball not in play is accidentally dislodged from the tee, or falls off before the player makes a stroke at it, there is no penalty (Rule 11). Nor is there a penalty if a stroke has been made at the ball, but the stroke counts.

and you can't therefore incur a penalty if it moves. A stroke is defined as a forward movement of the club with the intention of striking the ball **(Definitions)**. The bit about intending to strike the ball covers you if you make a practice swing, for example, and hit the ground, causing the ball to fall off the tee. But, of course, you know better than to make practice swings on the tee anyway."

George, who had known no such thing, nodded wisely and said: "So until I make an honest attempt to hit the ball from the teeing ground, the ball is not in play and I can't incur a penalty if it moves."

Ball moving at address

"Exactly," said the captain, by which time they had reached George's ball and he surveyed his shot. "But once the ball is in play that's an entirely different matter. Through the green, if the ball moves after you have addressed it, you are deemed to be at fault and you incur a penalty stroke under **Rule 18-2b**."

George, thinking he had seen a loophole in the Rules for the first time that day, said: "But who is to decide if I have addressed the ball, surely that is a matter of opinion and I could, for example, say: 'No, I haven't addressed it, I was just settling into position'."

"I'm afraid you can't, because the Rules even define when the ball has been addressed. Through the green, you have addressed it once you have taken up your stance and grounded the club behind the ball. In a hazard, it is as soon as you have taken up your stance because, as we are both tired of hearing by now, you cannot ground your club in a hazard."

"OK," said George, "so what if, through the green, I never ground my club? If I did that, then presumably I could never fall foul of **Rule 18-2b**."

To George's surprise, the captain agreed: "You're absolutely right and I regularly play with a chap who never grounds his club for that very reason. I tried it myself for a while but I just couldn't get on with it. I kept topping it."

George was by now ready to play and hit a solid shot that came up about 90 yards short of the green. When they reached the captain's ball he assessed his shot and addressed the ball by taking up his stance and grounding the club. Just as he was about to start his backswing a gust of wind came up which caused his ball to rock; it moved slightly and then settled back into its original position.

The two men exchanged glances and the captain smiled and said: "Don't say anything, George, I can read your mind. And I know that it seems you've been getting the rough end of the Rules today and they seem to have been working to my advantage most of the time, but in this instance I have not incurred a penalty, or at least I don't think I have.

"According to the Definitions, a ball has moved if it leaves its position and comes to rest in any other place. But if it moves and settles back in its original position it is not considered to have moved. Now this is an area where we all have to be honest and the temptation is very great to think that a ball has settled back in its original spot, especially when you consider that if it hasn't, we incur a penalty, often through no fault of our own. However, in this instance I honestly don't believe that the ball has moved,

Opposite: Remember that if you should brush the sand in a bunker with your club during the backswing, you will incur two penalty strokes for grounding your club in a hazard.

according to the Rules, but if you believe otherwise I will happily accept your judgement.''

George, however, agreed completely with the captain and they continued playing the hole.

One of the reasons why many golfers do not ground their clubs in the rough when taking up their stance is to avoid falling foul of **Rule 18**. When the ball is sitting in or on long grass, touching the grass behind it can cause it to move so, in these situations, it is as well to get into the habit of not grounding the club. Should the ball move when you address it, the ball should be replaced.

Building a stance

When George reached his ball he found that it was on the side of a slope, with the ball above his feet. "I always have trouble playing these shots and feel that I want to stand on something to make me a bit taller and the shot a bit easier," he said.

"But of course, you never would," Edward replied, "because that would be illegal as you are not allowed to build a stance **(Rule 13-3)**. You are allowed to place your feet firmly in taking a stance but that's all. The American pro Craig Stadler fell foul of this rule a few years ago. His ball was under a bush and he decided to play it from his knees. But because the ground was wet and muddy, and he didn't want to get his trousers dirty he knelt on a towel. He was seen and penalized for breaking **Rule 13-3**."

Considerably enlightened, George continued playing the hole without incident, he and the captain both taking fives.

Key points

1 A ball is not in play on the teeing ground until a player makes a stroke with the intention of playing at and fairly striking the ball.
2 Through the green, a player has addressed the ball if he adopts his stance and grounds the club.
3 In a hazard, a player has addressed the ball after he has taken up his stance.
4 In either situation, if the ball moves after the player has addressed it, he incurs a penalty stroke.
5 If the ball settles back into its original position it is not considered to have moved.
6 If the ball does move, it shall be replaced.

The thirteenth hole

When they reached the 13th hole, a par 4 of 372 yards, both men were restored to their normally good spirits, so much so that the captain decided to tell George an old golfing joke.

"It was in heaven where God and St Peter decided to have a round of golf at the spiritual peace links — a contradiction in terms if ever there was one but there you go," the captain began. "St Peter, who was a very keen golfer — all decked out in the latest sweater, fashionable shoes and so on — got on the first tee and hit a good solid drive down the middle, using his new carbon shafted, peripheral weighted, turbo charged driver.

"God, who looked as if he was wearing a 70-year-old gardener's cast-off clothes, got a battered old wooden club from his decrepit canvas bag and hit an appalling shot — topped it so badly that it barely rolled off the front of the tee. But just as

Below: If a dog or other outside agency runs off with your ball after it has come to rest, you must take a drop, without penalty, as near as possible to the point from which it was taken.

it was about to stop moving a magnificent golden eagle swooped from the sky, clutched the ball in its talons and flew off up the fairway. As it was crossing the green a bolt of lightning rent the sky and hit the eagle broadside on, killing it stone dead, whereupon it dropped the ball which bounced on the green and rolled straight into the hole for an ace.

"St Peter looked at God and said: 'Are you going to mess about all day or have you come here to play golf?'"

George dutifully chuckled in appreciation and as they were walking up the fairway he said: "But in all seriousness, what would have been the ruling in that joke; would the hole-in-one have stood?"

Outside agencies

"Yes it would. You see, the eagle would be defined by what the legislators of golf call an outside agency, something that is not, in effect, part of the game. That term also includes other people who might be around, like a referee, marker, spectator, man out walking his dog or courting couple embracing in the undergrowth. The important thing to remember about the joke is that the ball had not come to rest when the outside agency — in this case the eagle — deflected its path; therefore it is played where it comes to rest **(Rule 19-1)**.

"The general principle through the green is that if your ball has stopped moving before it is interfered with, replace it **(Rule 18)**. If it is still moving when the outside agency interferes, play it from wherever it comes to rest. Sometimes, of course, that isn't possible, such as . . ."

The captain never finished his sentence, shook his fist up the fairway and cried: "Hey, stop it."

George looked up in time to see a small boy scamper into the bushes, clutching the captain's golf ball.

"The cheeky little monkey," George said, adding after a moment's thought: "I say, Edward, does he constitute an outside agency?"

"Yes, he does, and if I ever get my hands on him he will be a sore and regretful outside agency. Mind you, I may have lost a golf ball but at least I don't have to face the prospect of a penalty. My ball had obviously come to rest before he took it so I must replace by taking a drop as near as we can establish from where the lad took it — which is what I was about to explain when I spotted him. Mind you, as the ball was on the fairway and we saw it fairly clearly, replacing it shouldn't be too much of a problem.

"The rule is obviously a fair one — it would be far too harsh to be penalized for something over which you have no control. In fact, it is this rule that has given birth to the phrase 'a rub of the green'. The legislators of the game say that if your ball is moving and is deflected or stopped by an outside agency — as it was

Opposite top: This player's opponent's ball has come to rest against his trolley. The opponent is lucky: he does not incur a penalty (Rule 19) and he may elect to play the ball as it lies or replay his last stroke. Opposite below: Here the opponent is less lucky because his ball has come to rest against his own bag. In matchplay this is loss of hole; in strokeplay, a two-stroke penalty. The ball should be played as it lies unless it rests on or in his, his partner's or their caddies' clothes or equipment. If this happens, through the green, or in a hazard, he drops the ball. On the green he places it as near as possible to where it came to rest.

Above: You may at any time request that another player marks his ball on the putting surface.

in the joke — that is a 'rub of the green', which can be good or bad. But this principle does not apply on the green. There, if a ball in motion is interfered with by an outside agency, or comes to stop in or on an outside agency, the putt must be replayed."

One of the best known cases of interference by an outside agency happened a few years ago and Nick Faldo was the unwitting beneficiary. While playing the Australian Graham Marsh in the World Matchplay at Wentworth, Faldo's shot disappeared into the partisan crowds behind the 16th green and, after several seconds' pause, bounced back into a favourable position. It had clearly been

kicked or thrown back by one of the Englishman's supporters, who did not appreciate that he or she was doing Faldo more harm than good. He had no choice but to play the ball where it came to rest — he would have been penalized had he done anything different — but a regrettably sour taste spoiled his victory with the totally unfounded suggestion that Faldo had somehow behaved badly. In fact, although television viewers saw clearly what had happened, the players' view would have been obscured by a grass mound, so Faldo would have no idea what happened until he finished the match and someone told him.

When the captain had replaced without penalty and played his second shot, they moved to George's ball where he played the most sickening of all golf shots, the shank. His ball shot off at right angles but not very far. After two yards it struck the captain a direct hit on his left knee, whereupon he began hopping about, and cursing.

"Oh, Edward, I'm really sorry," said George.

"Don't worry, George," answered the captain, massaging his injury. "I shouldn't have been standing there in the first place."

After a few moments establishing that the damage was not permanent, he said: "In this instance, I am an outside agency so you play the ball where it lies or have the option of replaying the stroke. If you choose the latter you must replace the ball, not drop it, but actually I've done you a favour because your ball was heading for the rough. If, however, I had been your partner, or trolley, or any part of your equipment or either of your caddies, or even yourself, you would have been penalized two strokes **(Rule 19-2b)**."

George was puzzled by this explanation and said: "I'm a little confused. Why are you an outside agency now but not an outside agency if you were on my team?"

"It is an unfortunate necessity that the rule makers have had to develop a poor opinion of their fellow man," Edward explained. "Imagine, for example, that your caddie, or partner, was standing by the green in front of a water hazard and your ball, which you topped, was rolling towards the water. It wouldn't be too dificult for them to drop a golf bag or get in the way and claim that it was accidental."

After digesting this George played his next shot to the green, which he did with success. He was furthest from the hole and the captain asked if he should mark his ball but George said: "That's OK. I don't think I'll be going that far to the right." How little he knew. When he made his stroke the putter head caught the ground first, twisting off line and sending George's ball straight for that of the captain, which it struck full on.

Striking another ball on the green

"Well, I'm sorry, George, but that means a two-stroke penalty for you **(Rule 19-5)**," the captain said. "If we were anywhere else on the hole there would be no penalty but there is on the green because you may always request that another ball be marked on the green. The good news is that you don't have to replay the stroke but must play it from where it lies."

Under the circumstances George did well to hole out with his next putt for a total of seven (drive, shanked approach, third onto the green, first putt, two-stroke penalty and second putt). The captain, having the advantage of seeing the line of George's second putt, single putted for a birdie three.

■■■ Key points ■■■

1 An outside agency is any agency that is not part of a match or a competitor's side. Wind and water are not outside agencies.
2 If a moving ball is deflected or stopped by an outside agency it is a rub of the green and the ball is played as it lies.
3 If a stationary ball is moved by an outside agency, the ball is replaced.
4 If the ball cannot be recovered, another may be substituted.
5 If your ball, played from the green, touches another on the green you incur a two-stroke penalty.

The fourteenth hole

As they moved to the 14th, a 507 yard par 5 hole, George said: "Everything you say makes perfect sense and, while some of the Rules seem harsh, I cannot argue with the logic of them. But something I've always had difficulty with is penalties and dropping and placing.

"Sometimes, for example, I get penalized two strokes; sometimes I get penalized one. And I never can remember under which circumstances I should drop the ball, and under which ones I should replace it, and whether I can clean the ball while I'm at it."

The captain replied: "Why don't we take a few minutes on this bench, and let the following match through while I go over those very points?"

Accidentally breaking a rule

After they had settled down, Edward said: "Many people have tried to classify the penalties under brief headings but there are a lot of difficulties with this approach because the Rules themselves have a certain inconsistency. My own system is to think of three broad categories. First is 'accidental' shots; this would include an air shot, the ball falling off the tee after you have started your stroke, and the ball moving when you address it, as costing one stroke. My second category is 'buying yourself out of trouble', exchanging a stroke for a hopefully improved position. Here, for example, you might declare your ball unplayable and take a drop away from

the trouble at a one-stroke penalty. Or your ball may be visible in a water hazard but you decide not to try and play it, in which case the same applies. The third category is unwittingly or accidentally breaking a rule of golf, in which case you are penalized two strokes in strokeplay, loss of hole in matchplay. So, for example, if you accidentally grounded your club in a hazard, that would be a two-stroke penalty."

Deliberately breaking a rule

"If you deliberately break a rule," the captain continued, "that is a serious transgression and you would be subject to disqualification, and quite possibly even more punishment, such as being thrown out of the club. Because golf is a self-regulating game we have to be absolutely honest with ourselves and often you are the only one who will know whether you have broken a rule or not. Of course, some offences, like surreptitiously dropping an extra golf ball down the leg of your trousers, can only be deliberate attempts to cheat and in such

Opposite: A ball that comes to rest on or in a movable obstruction may be lifted, the obstruction moved and, through the green or in a hazard, the ball is dropped as near as possible to the point directly under the obstruction where the ball lay, no nearer the hole. On the green, the ball is placed, not dropped. It may be cleaned when lifted.

circumstances the committee of the club would take the worst possible view. I would be very surprised if someone caught in such an act would be allowed to remain a member.

"So, for accidentally breaking a rule you get a two-stroke penalty. But the 'one stroke offences', in many instances, are not really offences. They are within the rules and the penalty stroke represents a way of buying yourself out of an impossible situation. It's like the 'Get out of Jail Free' card in Monopoly, except it isn't free, it costs a stroke. Mind you, this is not a hard and fast rule so just bear it in mind as a general guide."

Dropping and placing

"Your second point, concerning dropping and placing," said the captain, "is quite logical, which is probably what you were coming to expect by now. In simple terms, if you are able to replace, you do; if not, you drop. If your ball was plugged

Above and opposite: Having marked as near as possible on the green, the player removes the obstruction and then places the ball.

in the fairway it would be impossible to replace it in exactly the same spot without recreating the conditions from which you are seeking relief. Therefore you drop. Equally, if your ball comes to rest near a movable obstruction and, while taking the obstruction away the ball moves, you would replace the ball. But if it comes to rest on the same obstruction, an empty potato chip packet, for example, you would not be able to reproduce exactly its lie once you take the packet away, so you drop. The exception to this is on the green where, after removing the packet, you replace the ball as near as possible to where it lay on the obstruction, but no nearer the hole. Again, the reason for that is fairly obvious: the legislators of golf do not want to see unnecessary pitch marks being made in greens so on the putting surfaces you always replace, never drop. Another thing to remember is that if your ball is to be replaced, you must mark it before lifting.

Cleaning the ball

"And for your final point, you can clean the ball any time you lift it under the Rules, with three exceptions **(Rule 21)**. The first exception is if you are lifting it to see if it is unfit for play **(Rule 5-3)**. The second is if you are lifting it for identification **(Rule 12-2)** and in this case you can only clean it enough to enable you to identify it. And the third is if the ball is interfering with or assisting play **(Rule 22)**. For example, if our golf balls were lying side by side on the fairway, or your ball was lying in the spot where I wanted to take up my stance, I could ask you to lift it."

In the time it took the captain to complete this explanation the match that had been following was now well up the fairway so he and George continued their round.

Dropping the ball

After both had hit good drives they strolled up the fairway and George said: "Another thing I get confused about is one club and two club lengths when I'm dropping the ball. What's the rule of thumb here?"

"That's the easiest one you've asked me all day," Edward replied. "If you have declared your ball unplayable, or you are exercising one of your options

from a lateral water hazard, then you measure two club lengths; in all other circumstances, it's one club length. An easy way that most people remember is that one club length (dropping away from casual water, dropping off the wrong green and so on), is without penalty. But two club lengths (ball unplayable or dropping out of a lateral water hazard) is with a penalty.

"In either case, once the ball strikes the ground it can roll up to a further two club lengths away. The permitted way of dropping, as you know, is to stand with the arm outstretched at shoulder height. There are situations in which you must re-drop but they are fairly obvious. If you are in a hazard you must drop in the hazard, so if the ball rolls back onto the fairway, then you re-drop. Equally, if you are on the fairway and the ball rolls into a bunker, then you re-drop onto the fairway. Also, if the ball rolls onto a putting green, or out-of-bounds, or back into the situation from which you are taking relief, you should re-drop **(Rule 20-2c)**.

"The crucial bits to remember are that when you have dropped, whether within one or two club lengths, the ball can then roll up to a further two club lengths away, as long as it goes no nearer the hole. The other clauses that I've just mentioned, about hazards, OB and so on, are because the intention is that you should drop into the sort of terrain where the ball came to rest. Therefore, if it comes to rest in a bunker, drop in a bunker; if it comes to rest in bounds, drop in bounds, and so on. But here you must remember our old definition 'through the green', which makes no distinction between fairway, rough and other parts of the course. If you are in the fairway and the ball rolls into the rough; tough luck. If it happens

the other way round, count your blessings.

"One final point about dropping the ball. If you drop twice and the ball rolls more than two club lengths away, or into a bunker or whatever, you can, after the second failed attempt, place the ball."

After this lengthy explanation, both men were glad to get on with the golf and played the hole without incident; Edward taking five, George, six.

▬▬▬ Key points ▬▬▬

1 Deliberately breaking a rule may lead to disqualification.
2 Unwittingly breaking a rule usually invokes a two-stroke penalty in strokeplay, loss of hole in matchplay.
3 A one-stroke penalty is often a price to be paid for getting out of trouble, or the penalty for a 'ghost' shot.
4 If the ball can be replaced in its identical position, do so; if not, drop it.
5 A ball is dropped within one club length of the nearest point of relief and may roll up to a further two club lengths away.
6 The only exceptions to this are dropping from an unplayable lie or from a lateral water hazard. In these instances you may drop within two club lengths and again the ball may roll up to a further two club lengths away, no nearer the hole.

The fifteenth hole

The 15th hole, at 189 yards, was another of George's bogey holes — in eight attempts he had never found the green. Edward who still had the honour, hit an excellent long iron shot that finished within feet of the flag. George, assuming the unlikelihood of lightning striking twice, was convinced before he addressed the ball that he would not hit a good shot. He didn't. His ball plunged into soft grass short of the green and, ominously, disappeared.

Ball in its own pitch mark

When the two men reached the spot it was to discover that the ball had 'plugged', become embedded in its own pitch mark. George, who by now was enjoying his crash course in the Rules of Golf, said: "Don't say anything, Edward. Let me see if I can work this out for myself. The ball is not in casual water, although the ground is soft, nor is it in or touching a rabbit scrape, a hole made by a burrowing animal, or GUR, so I can't take relief under **Rule 25**.

"Now I know that the principles embodied in the Rules are that you hit the ball, find it and hit it again but that you should be entitled to the lie that your shot gave you. Therefore, in this instance, I presume that I just have to bite the bullet and play my next shot from this plugged lie."

The captain smiled and said: "That is admirably worked out, George, and completely wrong. **Rule 25-2** says that a ball embedded in its own pitch mark through the green in any closely mown area may be lifted, cleaned and dropped, without penalty, as near as possible to the spot where it lay but no nearer the hole. While we're discussing this it is worth taking a few minutes to talk about the meaning of 'through the green', a phrase that crops up in the Rules several times. Originally, the Rules made no mention of fairways, they just talked about 'through the green'. This referred to any part of the course that was not a teeing ground, green, hazard or water hazard.

"More recently they mention 'closely mown areas' which is accepted as being any part of the course, including paths through the rough, cut to fairway height or less. Therefore, in closely mown areas through the green you may lift, clean and drop an embedded ball, as near as possible to where it lay but not nearer the hole. Frankly, I think it's one of the more stupid rules of golf, or at least the bit about dropping is. If the ground is very soft it seems silly to drop from shoulder height when it could be just as simple to place the ball, without running the risk of creating another pitch mark, or even becoming embedded again. While I'm on this hobby horse, it seems equally stupid to me that you have to drop in a bunker when taking relief from, for example, casual water. Again, I would have thought it much better to allow us to place.

"Anyway, to return to the matter at hand, you now know that you can get free relief from a ball embedded in its own pitch mark in closely mown areas but it's always worth checking the clubhouse notice board as well because the committee has the right to make a local rule allowing a similar free drop from areas that are not closely mown. To you and me that means any part of the course other than teeing grounds, greens, hazards, water hazards and fairways or aprons of greens, in short, what we call the rough. If possible the committee should indicate which part of the course is covered by such a local rule but it could, in abnormal ground or weather conditions, extend to the whole course."

Ball on the wrong putting green

After following the procedure described by the captain, George played a horrible shot, a half shank that went 70 yards in the wrong direction and finished up on the fourth green. He looked at Edward who said: "Don't worry, the only penalty you get for that shot is that it is so far away from where you were aiming; you don't get penalized for landing on the wrong green **(Rule 25-3)**.

"What you have to do is find the point on the course nearest to where the ball lies that is not nearer the hole, not in a hazard and not on a green. Once you have identified that spot you may lift the ball,

Below and opposite: Through the green in a closely mown area, a ball embedded in its own pitch mark may be lifted, cleaned and dropped without penalty. It is advisable to mark it before you lift the ball. It should be dropped as near as possible to where it lay, no nearer the hole.

clean it and drop within one club length, without penalty. Unless prohibited by the committee, the 'wrong' putting green would include a practice green. Once again though, I must remind you that the nearest point of relief is exactly that; it is not the best point of relief. Therefore, if the ball was lying on the edge of the green near a copse of trees, you would have to take the drop in the trees.''

George was fortunate because his point of relief was in an advantageous spot. He played a good recovery onto the proper green and holed the putt for an unlikely four. The captain calmly stroked his birdie putt into the middle of the cup.

■■■■ Key points ■■■■

1 A ball embedded in its own pitchmark in closely mown grass may be lifted, cleaned and dropped, as near as possible to the spot where it lay, without penalty.
2 A ball on the wrong putting green may be dropped without penalty at the nearest point of relief that is not in a hazard, not on a green and is no nearer the hole.

16

The sixteenth hole

The 16th was another par 3, this time of 110 yards. As you may imagine, its lack of distance was compensated for by having a well guarded green.

The captain hit a good shot that found the heart of the green, not far from the hole. George hit one of his cleanest strikes of the day and watched, partly in anguish, as it soared across the putting surface and disappeared from sight.

When they reached it, the golfers discovered that it was on the rear apron of the green, in an area of mud not wet enough to be considered casual water, and not embedded in its own pitch mark.

Winter rules

The captain immediately said: "It's all right, George, we're playing winter rules. You remember earlier that I said I had checked the notice board for local rules and it was then that I noticed that winter rules are still in operation. What happens is that if winter rules apply you can move or lift your ball, clean it and place it within six inches, no nearer the hole. But this only applies, of course, to closely mown areas. The idea behind the rule is

Right: If a sprinkler head lies between you and the flag, you are not entitled to relief. Opposite: But if the ball comes to rest in or near the sprinkler head, or it affects your stance or intended line of swing, you may drop, without penalty, within one club length of the nearest point of relief, no nearer the hole.

to acknowledge that in our climate you can often be left with an awful lie in winter in the middle of the fairway, so this is a way of avoiding that.

"It's always a good idea to check the notice board in the clubhouse before you start a round of golf; you never know what helpful information you might learn."

George replied: "But why don't they print the winter rules on the scorecard, like the one saying we can remove stones from bunkers?"

"Because a winter rule is meant to be temporary, and only applied when the ground conditions warrant it. But what tends to happen is that many clubs in the UK have a blanket policy of applying

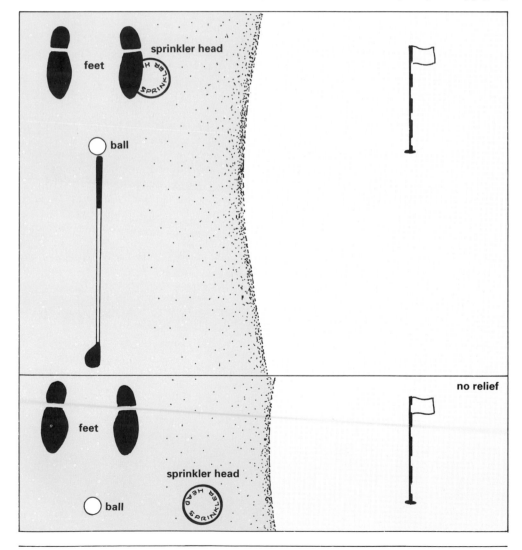

winter rules between, say, November 1 and March 31. It saves them having to keep putting up and taking down notices as conditions change, and it saves us getting confused about when the winter rules are in force. Can you imagine the confusion on a day like today, with the monthly medal being played, if half the field were moving their golf balls on the fairway all day, only to get back to the clubhouse and discover that no winter rules were in operation?"

George could. Having moved his ball within the permitted six inches he prepared to play a chip back to the green when the captain stopped him.

"Wait a minute, I hate to interrupt but I notice that you're going to play a bump and run shot with that 6-iron and that fixed sprinkler head on the edge of the green is right in line. You may be able to get relief, you know. Let's check."

Fixed sprinkler heads

The captain got out his scorecard and read: "'All fixed sprinkler heads are immovable obstructions and relief from interference by them may be obtained under **Rule 24-2.**' Well, we know that. 'In addition, if such an obstruction on or within two club lengths of the putting green of the hole being played intervenes on the line of play between the ball and the hole, the player may obtain relief, without penalty.' I thought as much. It says here that if the ball lies off the putting green, not in a hazard, and is

Opposite: If you are off the green and a sprinkler head is between you and the hole, tough! But if it interferes with your stance or intended line of swing you may drop without penalty within a club length of the nearest point of relief, no nearer the hole.

within two club lengths of the intervening obstruction, it may be lifted, cleaned and dropped at the nearest point to where it lay which is not nearer the hole, avoids interference and is not in a hazard or on a green.''

George was looking decidedly confused so the captain said: "First thing we must do is to see if the sprinkler head is within two club lengths of the green, and it clearly is. We don't even have to measure in order to see that. The second thing is to establish whether it's on the line between your ball and the hole, and again that's easy to confirm. Finally, we have to see if your ball is within two club lengths of the sprinkler head."

Using George's driver they measured the distance and discovered that the ball was within two club lengths of the sprinkler, thereby entitling George to a drop without penalty, no nearer the hole, not on a green and not in a hazard. Having completed this procedure he played a good bump and run that disappeared into the hole, for a birdie two.

Not to be outdone, Edward holed his putt for the same score.

◼◼◼◼ Key points ◼◼◼◼

1 Always check the clubhouse notice board and the scorecard to find out which local rules may be in play.

2 'Winter rules' allow for the ball, in closely mown grass, to be moved or placed within six inches, no nearer the hole.

3 Fixed sprinkler heads are often the subject of extra local rules.

The seventeenth hole

The 17th hole was a dog-leg par 4 of 372 yards. The captain took an iron from his bag and played a conservative shot into the fairway, about 195 yards out.

George immediately said: "That was an interesting choice of shot. I can see that you took an iron for safety because the hole is not very long but what club did you hit?"

From the way the captain groaned and shook his head, George could tell that he had made a mistake but was puzzled as to what this could be. "All right, Edward," he said, "I know I've done something wrong, tell me what the penalty is."

Seeking and giving advice

"Well, I'm sorry but you have incurred another two-stroke penalty," said the captain. "**Rule 8** prohibits us from giving advice to anyone but our partner, or seeking advice from anyone but our partner or our respective caddies. 'Advice' is defined as 'any counsel or suggestion, which could be influential on a player in determining his play, in choosing a club or the method of making a stroke. Giving information on the Rules or on matters of public information, such as the position of hazards or the flagstick on the putting green, is not advice. If we were playing matchplay you would have lost the hole before striking a ball."

The most notorious example of this rule being applied occurred in the 1971 Ryder Cup match in America. Bernard Gallacher and Peter Oosterhuis were paired for Great Britain and Ireland against Americans Arnold Palmer and Gardner Dickinson. On a par 3 hole, Palmer hit an iron to the green and Gallacher's caddie, one of several college students drafted in for the week, said: "Great shot, what did you hit?" A referee overheard the question and, after much deliberation, Gallacher and Oosterhuis were adjudged to have been in breach of **Rule 8** and they consequently lost the hole.

George eventually drove and watched his ball come to rest near the captain's. Their next shot, to the green, was 'blind' as it involved playing over the crown of a hill to a flag and hole they could not see. It was George's turn to play first and, as he had little idea where the flag was, he lined himself up on the middle of the hill. But before he could take the club back, Edward said: "I know you don't want to ask advice, George, especially after what happened on the tee, but I happen to know that the flag is on the right side of the green today. I checked it when we played the third hole earlier on, and I'm perfectly entitled to tell you.

"If you think about it, advising you

Opposite: Giving advice in matters such as club selection is not allowed (Rule 8). The player on the right will be penalized two strokes in strokeplay, loss of hole in matchplay, because he is preventing his fellow golfer from selecting a particular club, suggesting it to be the wrong one.

about club selection, or how to play a particular shot, could give you an advantage. But the location of the flag, or whether or not there's out-of-bounds behind the green, or a pond in front of it, is public knowledge, so I'm allowed to share that with you.

"In fact, this hole offers a good example of what I'm talking about. If I felt like the walk, or just doing you a favour, I could go to the brow of that hummock and stand directly between you

Above: Anyone can indicate the line of play to a player (Rule 8).

and the flag to show you what line to hit. Except on the green, anyone can indicate the line of play to you. But, and it's an important 'but', they must move well away from that line before you take your shot.

"The exception to that involves the flagstick. Again, if I was feeling energetic enough, I could walk to the green and hold the flagstick up to show you the

location of the hole **(Rule 17-1)**. However, such actions can only be taken on your authority but if someone holds up the flagstick and you don't object, it is assumed that your authority has been given. The reason for this is that if the ball strikes the flagstick while it is being

Above: However, they must not stand on or close to the line of play while the stroke is being played.

attended you receive a two-stroke penalty so it is only fair that you authorize such actions first.''

If someone were to indicate the line of play to George by standing on the hill, clearly it would be sensible for him to fix a second reference point in his mind's eye in relation to them. Then, when that person had moved away, he could focus on that second reference point — a tree in the background, for example, in order to play the shot.

Both players hit fine shots into the green. As he was lining up his putt, the captain asked George to tend the flag but before he putted he straightened up from his crouched position over the ball and said: "As we are fellow competitors in strokeplay I cannot ask your advice on the line of a putt. If we were partners, or you were my, or my partner's, caddie, I could.

"But if you are indicating the line of a putt, be very careful never to touch the green with your putter, the flagstick or anything else because that also would be a two-stroke penalty. The rationale behind that, I believe, is that a putter head placed on the grass may leave a mark for several minutes, particularly if there is dew."

The captain two putted but George went one better, taking three strokes to Edward's four.

Practice on the course

As they were moving to the final tee, they saw that the group ahead had just emerged from the trees, where they had clearly been searching for a ball. Edward said: "We'll have to wait a couple of minutes and there's no-one behind us so we might as well practise putting."

"But is that allowed?" George enquired. "I seem to remember reading somewhere that you couldn't practise during the course of a round."

"You can't," Edward replied, "at least, not while you're playing in the round. The only exception allows us to practise putting and chipping on the green we've just completed, the tee we're about to move onto, or a practice green. But that's all. We are not allowed to practise from a hazard or unduly delay play. And we certainly can't practise full shots, so if you had an old ball in your bag and decided to smash it into those trees, that would be a two-stroke penalty or loss of hole in matchplay. But even worse, if either of us had practised on the course earlier today, the day of the competition, or tested the surface of any putting green before starting our round, we would have been disqualified."

Key points

1 You may not seek advice in competition from anyone but your partner or either of your caddies; you cannot give advice to anyone but your partner.
2 Information on the Rules or matters of public knowledge, such as the location of the flagstick, or hazards, is not advice.
3 The flagstick may be held up at any time to indicate the location of the hole.
4 The line of play may be indicated at any time but the person showing the line must move away before the shot is played.
5 If the line of a putt is indicated, the ground must not be touched.
6 The only practice allowed on the course is between holes, chipping and putting.

The eighteenth hole

When they arrived at the tee of the 18th hole, a 398 yard par 4, both men felt that it had been a long time since they teed off. They once again both hit good drives and as they were walking up the fairway, George said: "I consider myself very fortunate to have played with you today, Edward, and I hope that I will absorb some of the information you have been kind enough to pass on. But what happens if I don't know a rule, or myself and my fellow competitor get into an argument over the interpretation of a rule, or simply that something happens that has never happened before, and is therefore not covered?"

Disputes, decisions and equity

"Well, I'll take your points one at a time," the captain replied. "If you don't know a rule, tough luck. Ignorance of law is no excuse in the courts and the same happens on a golf course. If you break a rule because you didn't know it existed, you still pay the penalty.

"In situations where there is an argument about procedure you proceed differently depending on whether you are playing matchplay or strokeplay. In matchplay any disputes must be settled before the hole is completed **(Rule 2-5)**. This does not mean that the players have to agree, merely to settle. Ideally, a referee can be called to offer a ruling then and there but if this is not possible, the player who is in disagreement says clearly to his opponent that he wishes to make

a claim and they then complete the hole. When the match is over they seek an official ruling.

"If a dispute occurs in strokeplay that nobody can settle, you are allowed to put a second ball into play and finish the hole, playing both balls. If you do not nominate which ball you wish to count, the score with the original ball will count assuming, of course, that its play has been legal.

"Finally, if a situation occurs that is not covered by a rule, they have a rule to cover it! **Rule 1-4** stipulates that if any point in dispute is not covered by the Rules, the decision shall be made in accordance with equity. This means, in effect, in keeping with natural justice, or fairness."

The players played out the hole, George taking a bogey five, Edward making a steady par four. After shaking hands and moving away from the green in preparation for checking and signing their scorecards, the captain said: "I must have a close look at that putter of yours, George; it's been intriguing me."

"By all means", George replied. "I borrowed it from a friend the other day, who also lent me a specialist wedge, and I couldn't decide until we teed off which ones to use. But I tried them both on the first hole and they seemed to work so I stuck with them."

George stopped as he noticed the look on the captain's face, which had turned a sickly green colour.

"And did you take your own clubs out

before playing?'' he asked.

"Why, no,'' George said. "Should I have?''

Permitted number of clubs

The captain said nothing but started counting the clubs in George's bag. He then counted them a second time and said: "I'm very sorry, George, but that's a four-stroke penalty. You are only allowed to carry a maximum of fourteen clubs and you have fifteen in your bag. You are therefore penalized two strokes for each hole you played with the wrong number, but there is a maximum four-stroke penalty in any round. Therefore you incur the maximum penalty of four.

"If you start with fourteen clubs and one breaks accidentally then you can replace it. If you break it deliberately, by slamming it into the ground in anger, you cannot replace it. Had you noticed the extra club in your bag at the beginning of the round you could declare it was there but not use it for the duration of that round, which would have been OK. The legislators think it's perfectly acceptable for you to carry more than fourteen clubs as long as you don't use them. I'm sorry but there's nothing else I can say.''

To his surprise, George was not at all flustered and he said: "Don't worry, Edward. I've enjoyed the day and hopefully learned a lot — my score was never going to be brilliant anyway. Including all my penalty strokes, I've taken 103 strokes, which is nine over the 94 that I should shoot off my 22 handicap. And you took 81, which included a 10 on the 11th but that is still playing to handicap so you've had a good day.

"And don't forget, I do have a hole-in-one to remember.''

"Of course,'' said Edward, "which means that you owe me, and the rest of the clubhouse, a drink!''

Scorecard

Hole	Yards	Par	George	Edward
1	403	4	7	4
2	175	3	8	2
3	380	4	5	4
4	498	5	7	7
5	375	4	6	4
6	398	4	5	4
7	410	4	4	7
8	180	3	1	4
9	498	5	6	6
	3317	36	49	42

Hole	Yards	Par	George	Edward
10	410	4	14	4
11	392	4	4	10
12	480	5	5	5
13	372	4	7	3
14	507	5	6	5
15	189	3	4	2
16	110	3	2	2
17	372	4	3	4
18	398	4	5	4
	3230	36	54	39
Totals	6547	72	103	81

Index

All numerals in *italics* refer to illustrations

A

Accidentally breaking a rule, 74
Address, ball moving at, 66-68
Advice, seeking and giving, 86-90
Agency, outside, 70-72
American Masters, 26
Animals, burrowing, *44*, 45, 62, 79
Artificial obstructions, 36, 38, 40

B

Ball(s),
  in casual water, 41-42
  cleaning and repairing, 19-20, *62*, 77
  dropping, *11*, 76-78
  against golf bag, *71*
  identifying, *13*, *61*, 62, *63*
  in a lateral water hazard, 33-35
  lost, 12, 13-17, *60*
  marking, *20*, 62
    on putting green, *73*
  moving at address, 66-68
  moving in play, 63
  not in play on the teeing ground, 65-66
  overhanging hole, *23*
  in its own pitch mark, 79-80, *80*, *81*
  placing, 76
  provisional, 10-12, 60
  side by side in a hazard, *52*, 54
  standing on, 63, *64*
  striking another ball, 72-73
  against trolley, *71*
  unplayable, 13-17, 39, 78

in a water hazard, 29
on the wrong putting green, 80-81
Bird's nest, 40
Branches, 63,
Bunker(s), 27, 45
  balls side by side in, *52*, 54, 55-59
  brushing the sand in, *56*
  casual water in, *37*, 57-59
  grass island within, *55*
  greenside, 55
  raking, 19, *47*, 59
  unplayable ball in, 16
Burrowing animals, *44*, 45, 62, 79

C

Casual water, 41-45, 79
  in a bunker, *37*, 57-59
  dropping in, 78
Chapman, Roger, 18
Chipping, 18
Choice of clubs, 86
Cleaning ball(s), 19-20, *62*, 77
Club(s),
  brushing sand in a bunker with, *56*
  choice of, 86
  grounding a, 29, *51*, 57, 59
  in a hazard, *67*
  number of, 91-92

D

Deliberately breaking a rule, 74-76
Dew, 41
Dickinson, Gardner, 86

Disqualification, 76, 78
Divots, replacing, 19, *48*, 49, *49*
  on the tee, 23
Drawing lots, 8
Dropping the ball, *11*, 76-78
  in a bunker, 45
  in casual water, 41-42, 57, 78
  in a lateral water hazard, 33-35
  from an unplayable lie, *17*
  in a water hazard, 29

E

Etiquette, 46-49, 60

F

Faldo, Nick, 36, 72
Fixed sprinkler heads, *84*, 85
Flagstick, 20-23, 49
  advising on location of, 88-89

G

Gallacher, Bernard, 86
Giving advice, 86-90
  on club selection, *87*
Green(s),
  damaging, 49
  striking another ball on, 72-73
Greenside bunkers, 55
Ground under repair, *44*, 45, 79
Grounding the club, 29
  in a hazard, *51*, 57, 59, *67*

H

Hazard(s), 50-54, 78, 79
  balls side by side in, 54
  dropping ball in, 78
  touching the ground in, *57*

water, 24-29, 41, 45
  lateral, 24, 30-35, 78
Holes, 45

I

Ice, 41
Identifying your ball, 13, 16, *61*, 62, *62*
  in leaves, 51
  lifting for, *63*
  in sand, 51
Immovable obstructions, 36, 38, 40
Impediments, loose, *21*, *38*, 39-40, 41, *50*, 51,
  52, 56, 63
Indicating line of putt, 90
Island within a bunker, *55*

J

James, Mark, 22
Jones, Steve, 26

L

Lateral water hazards, 24, 30-35, 78
Leaves, 51
Local rules, 83-84, 85
Long putters, 35
Loose impediments, *21*, 23, *38*, 39-40, 41,
  50, 51, 52, 56, 63
Lost ball, 12, 13-17
  identifying, 62
  looking for, *60*
  in a water hazard, 29

M

Marking the ball, *20*, *62*
  on the putting green, *73*
Marsh, Graham, 72
Measuring the teeing ground, *8*
Movable obstructions, 36, *75*, 76
Moving a ball in play, 63

O

Observing lifting and replacing ball, 62
Obstructions, 36-38, 40
    artificial, 36, 38, 40
    immovable, 36, 38, 40
    movable, 36, 38, 40, *75, 76, 76*
O'Connor Jnr, Christy, 26
Ogle, Brett, 18
Oosterhuis, Peter, 86
Out-of-bounds, *10*, 36, 40, 78
Outside agency, *69*, 70-72

P

Palmer, Arnold, 86
Pitch mark(s), 18-19, 23, 49
    ball in its own, 79-80, *80, 81*
    on the green, 76
Pitching, 18
Placing the ball, 76
Practice on the course, 90
Provisional ball, 10-12, 60
Putt, pointing out line of, *23*
Putter(s),
    leaning on, 49
    long, 35
Putting green,
    ball on the wrong, 80-81
    marking ball on, *73*

R

Raking bunkers, 19, *47*, 59
Relief without penalty, 45
    in casual water in a bunker, *59*
Removing the flagstick, 20-23, *21*
Repairing pitch marks, 18-19, 23, 49
Repairing spike marks, 18-19, 23, 49
Replacing balls, 19-20
Road Hole, 36
Rough, 78

Rule(s),
    accidentally breaking a, 74
    deliberately breaking a, 74-76
    local, 83-84, 85
    winter, 82-85

S

Scrapes, 45
Seeking advice, 86-90
Senior, Peter, 35
Snow, 41
Spike marks, 18-19, *19*, 49
    on line of intended putt, 23
Sprinkler heads, fixed, 82, *83, 84*, 85
Stance, taking up a, 62
Standing on ball, 63, *64*
Stewart, Payne, 36
Stroke and distance, 12, 16, 29, 33-34
Striking another ball on the green, 72-73

T

Taking up a stance, 62
Teeing ground, 79
    ball not in play on, *65*, 65-66
Teeing off, 8-10, *9*
Tending the flagstick, 20-23
Torrance, Sam, 21, 35

U

Unplayable ball, 13-17, 39, 78
    in a bunker, 16
Unplayable lie, dropping from, *17*

W

Water,
    casual, 41-45, 78, 79
    hazards, 24-29, 41, 45,
        lateral, 24, 30-35, 78
        unplayable ball in, 16
Winter rules, 82-85